Because It's All TRUE

Strategies for Thriving in Life & Faith

Rick Beckwith

ISBN: 978-1-967283-04-0 (Print)

Printed in USA

Dedication

To our wonderful grandchildren. You bring us more joy than you will ever know. Winnie and I love you to the moon and back! May you thrive in life as you follow Jesus all along the way.

Acknowledgements

I am eternally grateful for the inner circle of relationships who have blessed and shaped me throughout my life. I believe the old proverb to be true, that the character of a person can be seen in the company they keep.

I first want to thank my mother and father for their tireless love and godly example. They planted good seeds that would be watered later.

I'm thankful for Marty McGinn, my high school Young Life leader, who introduced me to a personal relationship with Jesus Christ, and showed me that following Jesus can be fun.

I thank God for Lee Corder, who, as the area director for Young Life in Montgomery County Maryland, recruited me to serve as a volunteer leader. He had vision for me I could not see myself, and he helped bring that vision to fruition. Lee also introduced me to the idea of a covenant friendship and has been one of those friends for over 40 years.

I'm thankful for my first boss, Chuck Reinhold, who introduced me to a set of guiding principles that still undergird my life. His love for the Scriptures and bold faith still inspire me.

When Pat and Betsy Goodman invited me to live with them for two years as a Young Life trainee, I witnessed what a Christ-centered marriage and family looked like in full bloom. Their missionary spirit, joy, and love set a high bar for me to run after. I've never reached that bar but I'm still in the battle!

Mike O'Leary hired me to my first national role in Young Life and taught me how to lead by influence rather than by line authority. Mike and Carol showed me how two very differently gifted people can form a dynamic team. Grateful for their friendship!

John Pascoe, Tim Weaver, Scot Henderson, Matt Milstead, and Lou Von Kahle – thank you for inviting me into your inner circle and committing to walk together in this lifelong journey with the Savior!

I'm grateful for the Spurs, Cougar B-team, and Band of Brothers for helping me "*Press on to know the Lord* (Hosea 6:3)."

I've been immeasurably blessed to walk with my best friend, John Colston, since the seventh grade. We have ministered side by side for more than four decades and aren't about to stop now. John keeps me balanced and focused as I would otherwise be a wild stallion!

I am indebted to my friends, J. Manning Herr and Rick Reiter, for writing chapters 20 and 24 respectively. Their expertise in their fields is of the highest caliber. I know you will appreciate their practical wisdom!

In 1986 I was introduced to the love of my life, my wife Kris. We met through a mutual friend and never looked back. I could not ask for a more faithful partner in life. We have been blessed with three wonderful daughters, all of whom are married, and we love and respect our sons in law.

To our grandchildren: Brady, Jo, Hadley, Rawlings, Nina, and Alfie, Winnie and Papa love you guys and can't wait to see how and where the Lord leads you. Thanks for putting up with my Dad Jokes!

Table of Contents

FOREWORD

Rick Beckwith has been a friend and mentor most of my adult life. We have labored together in the ministry of Young Life to introduce as many adolescents to Jesus as possible, and to help them grow in their faith.

This is where Rick shines. I have witnessed firsthand, in his role as Director of Discipleship, he trains leaders in strategies and practices to help young people grow in their faith for the long-haul. The principles for thriving in life Rick lays out in this book aren't just theory but he lives them out! When Rick speaks, people listen...because his actions speak louder than his words.

When I was starting out in my journey after college, a mentor shared that one of the keys to life is to see the eternal in the mundane. We need to see the extraordinary in the ordinary and the adventure in the everyday. Rick helps us do this in *Because It Is All True*. Following Jesus is meant to be an adventure, an explosion of life and beauty in the needy world, and herein lies not just a tool box but the entire tool shed for growing in Christ.

This book is a master class in discipleship with every chapter bursting with practical application. It's a "back to the basics" manual but also useful for seasoned veterans of the faith. It's challenging yet realistic. Chapter four that outlines a collection of Bible study methods alone is worth the price of the whole book.

Rick has often asked me for a prayer request and checked up on it soon after. When he says he prays for 400 people consistently, this is the amazing truth. I think that is one of the reasons Jesus has brought so much fruit from Rick's ministry. He takes II Timothy 2:2 as a life call to pass down the faith and be a faithful guide for those on their spiritual journey.

I am convinced that as you implement these practices in your life you will be drawn deeper into the arms of Jesus, and experience the exhilaration thriving brings. Whether you work through this book alone or with a small group you'll never be the same!

Peter Hardesty

Pete Hardesty currently lives near Washington DC and serves as the Vice President for Young Life College. He has a BA from the University of Virginia and a Master of Divinity from Reformed Theological Seminary.

Pete is co-author of the 2 Amazon #1 bestsellers: ADULTING 101 Book 1 and 2. Both of these books provide tools to help young people have wild success in the "real world." Book 3 is coming fall 2026 and will give the secrets to succeeding in leadership in the workplace in your 20's. He has been working with college students for over 25 years.

Pete is married to the love of his life, Giannina, and has a son Marcello, who is his favorite.

Introduction

Why I Wrote this Book

Thank you for picking up this book. I wrote it with you in mind and pray it will meet you on your personal journey toward the thriving life God intends for you. It is a natural sequel to my first book, "What if it's All True?" which was written to help seekers explore who Jesus is and what He intends for us in this life and the next. "Because It's All True" is written to help those of us who believe experience the fullness Jesus offers and not be sidetracked by frivolous pursuits.

What do I believe God desires for you and me?

Jesus said, *I have come that they might have life, and have it to the full* (John 10:10)! Contrary to the opinion of some, following Jesus is a thrill ride, not something mundane or restrictive. The Lord desires us to experience all that He made in creation, and the opportunities he puts in front of us each day. My journey with Jesus so far has been incredibly full, and I look forward to what awaits me with Him each day.

I have spent most of my adult life looking for the building blocks that will help young people construct a life that is full and fruitful; a life of thriving. I have served on the staff of Young Life for over forty years and worked with thousands of adolescents – the age group I still love most because they are full of life and are hope-filled about their future.

I have observed what it takes for someone who comes to Christ to build a foundation sufficient to withstand the onslaught of issues spiraling out of control in our culture. I fully believe that the principles, practices and strategies in this book will serve you well in your quest to be the man or woman God desires you to be.

Our Source for Thriving

As a follower of Jesus, I believe the Scriptures to be the most tried and true source to serve as a guide, so I rely heavily on them as I've never seen them fail. After all, if the Bible truly is the words of God, inspired by the Holy Spirit and recorded by the hands of men, then there is no more trustworthy source for guidance. Each chapter begins with a verse or two that sets the stage and gives authority to the principle to be taught. I urge you to read each passage carefully envisioning what the Lord desires to communicate to you. His Word is timeless and therefore is as relevant today as ever.

The Bible tells us there is a choice before each one of us – a choice no one can make for us. This choice will determine the direction and the outcome of our lives. How we choose will determine the lens through which we view life, the values that guide us, who we marry, the priorities we teach our children, and the legacy we leave in our wake. Ultimately, this decision will determine where we spend eternity. In His famous Sermon on the Mount, Jesus admonished His listeners to heed the following advice: *Enter through the narrow gate. For wide is the gate and broad is the road that leads to destruction, and many enter through it. But small is the gate and narrow the road that leads to life, and only a few find it* (Matthew 7:13-14).

The wise Old Testament prophet, Jeremiah, gives us some guidance in the choice before us – *This is what the Lord says: Cursed is the one who trusts in man, who draws strength from mere flesh and whose heart turns away from the Lord. That person will be like a bush in the wastelands; they will not see prosperity when it comes. They will dwell in the parched places of the desert, in a salt land where no one lives. But blessed is the one who trusts in the Lord, whose confidence is in him. They will be like a tree planted by the water that sends out its roots by the stream. It does not fear when heat comes; its leaves are always green. It has no worries in a year of drought and never fails to bear fruit* (Jeremiah 17:5-8).

Jeremiah highlights two options for seeking a life of thriving: The first is to trust in man and his ideas, and the alternative is to trust in God and His ideas. Given these two options, and their consequences, I suspect few would KNOWINGLY choose option one. However, for a number of reasons it seems a majority of the populous ends up there – not by intent, but due to subtle slippage and the deceptiveness of culture.

Like the early Hebrews, sadly, too many today will choose to do what seems right in their own eyes and strive to figure out their purpose as they see fit – detached from godly inspiration. They are (at least for the time-being) on the perilous road that leads to destruction. The Apostle Paul said this about these people: *They are darkened in their understanding and separated from the life of God because of the ignorance that is in them due to the hardening of their hearts* (Ephesians 4:18). John, the youngest of Jesus' disciples, gave this testimony from his personal experience: *The true light that gives light to everyone was coming into the world. He was in the world, and though the world was made through him, the world did not recognize him* (John 1:9-10). These words seem as true today as ever, don't they?

If you have chosen to follow Jesus you have made the most important decision in the world. And, following Jesus isn't just a good idea to add to our lives – it is the grandest idea! It demands our full commitment and allegiance. When we repent and realign ourselves to walk with our eyes fixed on Jesus, we become a new creation.

Baptism is an important outward expression of this inner reality. Galatians 3:27 says, *For all of you who were baptized into Christ have clothed yourselves with Christ.* When we submerge beneath the water in baptism it symbolizes our dying to our old self and the law of sin and death. Then we rise out of the water as a new creation fully clothed in the righteousness of Christ.

A "Yes" to Jesus also means becoming His child and being commissioned to carry out his work every day we have breath. Through this personal relationship with Jesus we begin to slowly take on the character of our Lord. As we connect with Him in the Scriptures and in prayer we start to see in a mirror the person we want to become. Jesus promises His presence through the Holy Spirit to everyone who accepts His gift of salvation. This radically impacts our perspective on life.

The process of growing in our relationship with Jesus is called, Sanctification. My good friends Will and Sandra Cravens purchased a new home in Florida just before hurricane Ian struck. Before they even moved in their house was destroyed. The outer shell looked the same but the inside had to be completely gutted and rebuilt. The end product will be a much more beautiful home than the original.

Similarly, those of us on a journey with Jesus are in the process of being sanctified. The old house is being torn down and a new and much better one is being constructed. Paul defined it this way: *Therefore, if anyone is in Christ they are a new creation. The old has gone, the new has come* (2 Corinthians 5:17). This book will highlight some of the wonderful features of our new dwelling, and offer instruction for making the house strong.

How to Maximize the Impact of This Book

This book is not written to be read through in a few sittings like a novel. Rather, each chapter stands alone and should be thoroughly digested before moving on to the next. I encourage you to ponder and take notes on the Questions to Consider that follow each chapter. And, since the journey of life is more fruitful when it is shared with close friends, I encourage you to invite a person or persons in your inner circle to work through this book with you. The discussion questions work well for small groups as well as individuals.

The first page of the appendix in the back is titled, "My Plan for Thriving." When processing each chapter, I encourage you to write an action step or two that you will incorporate into your strategy for experiencing the very best the Lord has for you. Make your action steps clear, specific, and measurable so you can observe your progress along the way. And don't rush. Work through this book at your own pace looking for application as the Spirit prompts you.

The principles and practices herein have stood the test of time and are transferable to each of our personal contexts. I have seen them at work in hundreds of people and attest to their impact on my own life. I trust your story, although truly unique, will be similarly positive! I pray you feel God's hand leading you as you journey through each chapter. Now jump in with eyes wide open – Because It's All True!

CHAPTER 1

The Call to Thrive

As long as he (Uzziah) sought the Lord,
God gave him success.
2 Chronicles 26:5b

Let's face it, people the world over desire lives of meaning, purpose, fulfillment, peace and oh yes, love. These qualities combine to equal Thriving, a term I define as "flourishing in one's personal relationships, goals, and purpose in life." Isn't this what we all long for? While we may envision celebrities, sports stars, or the very rich to be examples of thriving people, they are not the only ones for whom thriving is available. In fact, many of them are still searching for what would make them feel successful and complete. The reason thriving eludes us is because we too often seek an answer for the fulfillment of our desires in the wrong places.

In Mark 5, we see a picture of a man who is clearly NOT thriving. I would venture to say his life up to this point is the complete opposite of thriving. Here is his story…

When Jesus got out of the boat, a man with an impure spirit came from the tombs to meet him. This man lived in the tombs, and no one could bind him anymore, not even with a chain. For he had often been chained hand and foot, but he tore the chains apart and broke the irons on his feet. No one was strong enough to subdue him. Night and day among the tombs and in the hills he would cry out and cut himself with stones (Mark 5:2-5).

Bound by chains, feared by all, cut off from all who knew or loved him. What a sad picture. This is the work the devil desires – to do whatever it takes to keep us from Jesus and the thriving He offers. But Jesus overcame the best the devil could throw at him and He set this man free. Listen to what the townspeople saw following the healing of this formerly demon-possessed man: *...people went out to see what had happened. When they came to Jesus, they saw the man who had been possessed by the legion of demons, sitting there, dressed and in his right mind; and they were afraid* (Mark 5:14b-15). He had been set free to live!

The Source of True Thriving

Consider for a moment some of the struggles money and fame bring to people. While we may be jealous of their money would we really want the strife that seems to accompany fame?

The actor, Jim Carrey, once told an interviewer, "I think everybody should get rich and famous and have everything they ever dreamed of so they can see that that's not the answer."[1] In a similar vain, John D. Rockefeller, the world's first billionaire, was once asked by a reporter, "How much money is enough?" Rockefeller famously replied, "Just a little bit more!" Mr. Rockefeller unknowingly made a profound statement about the human condition. Our minds are wired to want…we want more, we want less, we want things to be different, we want to be thinner or have more hair – we want things to be better! We want more money, more time, more love, more vitality. Just a little bit more."[2]

Clearly, neither money nor fame, nor even career success guarantees thriving. So where is this elusive quality found? This will be the focus of the subsequent chapters of this book.

Listen to this short sampling of Scriptures that portray the Creator's heart for us; His children:

- *Then the Lord your God will make you most prosperous in all the work of your hands and in the fruit of your womb, the young of your livestock and the crops of your land. The Lord will again delight in you and make you prosperous, just as he delighted in your ancestors, <u>if you obey the Lord</u> your God and keep his commands and decrees that are written in this Book of the Law and turn to the Lord your God with all your heart and with all your soul* (Deuteronomy 30:9-10).

- *Observe what the Lord your God requires: Walk in obedience to him, and keep his decrees and commands, his laws and regulations, as written in the Law of Moses. Do this so that you may prosper in all you do and wherever you go* (1 Kings 2:3).

- *The righteous will flourish like a palm tree, they will grow like a cedar of Lebanon* (Psalm 92:12).

- *How priceless is your unfailing love, O God! People take refuge in the shadow of your wings. They feast on the abundance of your house; you give them drink from your river of delights. For with you is the fountain of life; in your light we see light* (Psalm 36:7-9).

The Apostle Paul sums up how I feel reading these verses – *What, then, shall we say in response to these things? If God is for us, who can be against us?* (Romans 8:31).

The Barna Group's research on human flourishing identified five dimensions of thriving people: Faith – Relationships – Vocation – Finances – Health.[3] The study found that people who are engaged in their faith and were active in church experience higher degrees of thriving, not just in the faith dimension, but in all five aspects of thriving. Why is this the case? I submit it is because God is the author of all five areas, and therefore He has wisdom to share about each with those who are willing to listen.

Bruce Scott was a mentor throughout my adult life. He founded an award-winning commercial construction company that he stewarded with Kingdom values. Bruce had many quotable sayings, but one I suspect he learned the hard way was: "If you get it wrong in the foundation it will follow you all the way to the roof." Our lives are like a house – if we build them on the right foundation, they will stand the test of time. But if the foundation is built on shaky ground, the house is destined to fall. Now, on to chapter 2.

Questions to Consider

1. Describe what thriving looks like to you?
2. Do you believe God wants you to thrive? Why or why not?
3. Can you point to some reasons why you have not experienced the level of thriving God intends for you?
4. What steps can you take to experience greater or more consistent thriving? Note these in My Plan for Thriving in the Appendix.

CHAPTER 2

Build a Firm Foundation

For no one can lay any foundation other than the one already laid, which is Jesus Christ.
1 Corinthians 3:11

In Him the whole building is joined together and rises to become a holy temple in the Lord. And in Him you too are being built together to become a dwelling in which God lives by His Spirit.
Ephesians 2:21-22

As mentioned in the close of chapter 1, foundations are critically important. Our neighbors found a crack in their foundation that quickly spread around the four sides of their home. Since these cracks were hidden behind drywall they could have gone unnoticed for quite some time. By the time they were discovered their house was in danger of caving in on them. Thankfully, radical repairs were made to sure up their home. From the outside, all looked fine. It was in the hidden depths of the foundation that things were woefully amiss.

At the close of Jesus' famous Sermon on the Mount he tells the following parable: *Therefore everyone who hears these words of mine and puts them into practice is like a wise man who built his house on the rock. The rain came down, the streams rose, and the winds blew and beat against that house; yet it did not fall, because it had its foundation on the rock. But everyone who hears these words of mine and does not put them into practice is like a foolish man who built his house on sand. The rain came down, the streams rose, and the winds blew and beat against that house, and it fell with a great crash* (Matthew 7:24-27).

What were the differences between the wise and foolish builders? Obviously, one chose a solid, immoveable foundation on which to build their home, while the other chose soil that is unstable. Palestine (where Jesus told this parable) is subject to violent rains and sudden floods. The Jordan River annually swells to dangerous levels as do the streams that run through the hills. Therefore, houses erected in this area needed to be anchored to rock to withstand these turbulent conditions.

So what would cause someone to choose to build on sand over rock? Perhaps it was easier to work with, required less engineering and time on the front end, or was less expensive. Not being a first-century, Palestinian I don't know! But long-term, most homebuilders then or now would agree that drilling deep into the bedrock and building on that foundation would make for the most secure and lasting structures.

Note another difference in these two builders: Without looking back at the text, do you think they both listened to the Word of God…?

The text says they did. The difference that impacted the whole of their lives was what they did with God's Word. One put it into practice while the other heard it and ignored it. Sadly, my experience tells me that by lunchtime Monday most Christians cannot recall the theme of the sermon preached the day before, and they certainly aren't putting it into practice. What is the principle to heed? Without clear application, impact is minimal.

Putting God's Word into practice is a hallmark of our follow up work in Young Life. In our Bible studies, we ask the students three types of questions:

a) Observation – simply repeating what is clearly stated in the text. These are nonthreatening questions anyone can answer.

b) Interpretation – this requires reading between the lines and interpreting what is going on. No right or wrong answers as these are more subjective.

c) Application – based on what you see and hear, how will you put God's Word into practice this week? Write down a measurable action you plan to take in faith. Then we begin our next Bible study by asking how their applications went – so they know we mean it!

It is in the application of God's Word that we become His hands and feet and see Him working both in and through us. The builder with the foundation on rock symbolizes the believer who puts Jesus in the center of every aspect of their life – their work, family life, social life, all of it! This is the privilege Jesus offers His followers – to walk with Him throughout every part of our day in a personal relationship. He not only serves as our guide but our cheerleader!

It is in the application of God's Word that we become His hands and feet and see Him working both in and through us.

Paul references Jesus as being the chief cornerstone - *In him the whole building is joined together and rises to become a holy temple in the Lord* (Ephesians 2:20-21). Jesus is the key foundation post for our lives. Anything else will be unsteady and fleeting.

The decision to follow Jesus brings with it another key component of our foundation; the gift of the Holy Spirit. The Holy Spirit fulfills a number of roles in our life, not the least of which is to guide us in the process of growing into the image of Christ; the process of sanctification mentioned earlier. What a gift to have the God of the Universe living in our heart! This is why Jesus told His disciples that it is to their advantage that He go away because that is when He will send the Advocate to be with them, and they will do even greater things than Him (John 16:7, 14:12).

Here is just a sampling of what Jesus offers His followers:

- Love
- Assurance/acceptance
- Clear Identity
- Complete forgiveness
- Guidance toward a thriving life
- Purpose
- Community blessing and impact
- Answered prayer
- Eternal life here and later
- Few regrets
- Joy and fulfillment

One builder put Jesus' words into practice and the other only heard it, then promptly ignored it. One trusted Jesus enough to follow Him obediently, whereas the other preferred to trust his or her own instincts. How did that work out for them? Because it's all true, we should be diligent to hear God's Word, know God's Word, understand God's Word, and yes, to obey God's Word as we walk it out in practice. The consequences for choosing otherwise are disastrous. With our foundation stone in place, let's keep building a life of thriving!

Questions to Consider

1. Why might someone choose an unstable foundation? Which of these reasons do you need to guard against?

2. What are the consequences of this choice?

3. Do you feel your spiritual foundation is solid? Is there an investment you can make soon to sure it up further?

4. How have you experienced putting God's Word into practice? How might you do so even more? Add your thoughts to My Plan for Thriving in the Appendix.

CHAPTER 3

Put Christ First

I have been crucified with Christ and I no longer live, but Christ lives in me. The life I now live in the body, I live by faith in the Son of God, who loved me and gave himself for me.
Galatians 2:20

Jesus said, Seek first his kingdom and his righteousness, and all these things will be given to you as well.
Matthew 6:33

It is easy to say that Jesus is our Lord and highest priority, but if we were to look at a diary of our daily activity how would our time expenditures support this claim? Even more convicting would be perusing a thought diary. Oy Vey!

One reason so many believers today let their faith subtly slip away is they don't understand what their commitment to Christ truly means. Jesus gave His all for our salvation, and He demands we be All-IN as well! Jesus challenged His disciples to count the costs of a commitment to him: *Suppose one of you wants to build a tower. Won't you first sit down and estimate the cost to see if you have enough money to complete it? For if you lay the foundation and are not able to finish it, everyone who sees it will ridicule you, saying, 'This person began to build and wasn't able to finish'* (Luke 14:28-30).

What are some of these costs? *Whoever wants to be my disciple must deny themselves and take up their cross daily and follow me* (Luke 9:23). Following Jesus isn't simply another activity to plug into our already full schedules. He demands our full allegiance; more precisely, our surrender. In return, we receive more than we could ever ask or imagine.

Jesus said, *No one who has left home or brothers or sisters or mother or father or children or fields for me and the gospel will fail to receive a hundred times as much in this present age: homes, brothers, sisters, mothers, children and fields—along with persecutions—and in the age to come eternal life* (Mark 10:29-30).

I would like to challenge us to consider the implications of a little Greek word used often in the gospels as it may have real significance to us. John 1:12 says, *Yet to all who did receive him, to those who believed in his name, he gave the right to become children of God.* Sounds pretty basic right? But, by believe, do you think John is merely talking about the intellectual acceptance of an idea; like, "I believe my car is blue?" No! I have great faith that my car is blue, but that belief has very little impact upon my daily life.

We are on a journey gradually being transformed into the image of Jesus.

The Greek word used here for "believe" is PIST-E-WO, which means: firm conviction; or to fully trust with everything we have! In other words, this form of belief should motivate our every thought, word and action. It should permeate every fabric of our lives! It should be our true north and define our purpose for living! Do you feel like you are growing in this sort of belief?

We are on a journey gradually being transformed into the image of Jesus. Our expectant participation speeds this process. Jesus left us with this promise: *Here I am! I stand at the door and knock. If anyone hears my voice and opens the door, I will come in and dine with them, and they with me* (Revelation 3:20). The abundant life awaits us as we allow our belief in Jesus to impact our thoughts, words, actions and relationships. What will it look like for you to be ALL IN with Jesus this year?

The Cost of the Wrong Thing in the Center

We live in an age of religious pluralism and moral relativism. A growing belief among Americans is that Heaven will be awarded good persons who follow any belief system they construct from the myriad of possibilities out there. However, the Bible teaches that, *Salvation is found in no one else, for there is no other name under heaven given to mankind by which we must be saved* (Acts 4:12). Jesus Himself boldly declared, *I am the way and the truth and the life. No one comes to the Father except through Me* (John 14:6).

At a pivotal moment in Jesus' journey with His disciples he asked them a poignant question: *Who do you say I am? Simon Peter answered, You are the Messiah, the Son of the living God. Jesus replied, Blessed are you, Simon son of Jonah, for this was not revealed to you by flesh and blood, but by my Father in heaven. And I tell you that you are Peter, and on this rock I will build my church, and the gates of Hades will not overcome it* (Matthew 16:15-18).

I know intellectually most of us would answer this question similarly to Peter. But is the full impact of this belief visible in every facet of our lives? Do our words, activities, relationships, and priorities reflect with integrity what we say we believe about Jesus? I wish I could say with Paul, *What is more, I consider everything a loss because of the surpassing worth of knowing Christ Jesus my Lord, for whose sake I have lost all things. I consider them garbage, that I may gain Christ* (Philippians 3:8). But alas, I am still a work in progress grateful for our Lord's patience!

It was prophesied hundreds of years before Jesus' birth that He would be rejected. Some reject Him outright, but more often, folks reject his authority by minimizing His true identity, and adhering only to the ideas that suit their whims or align with popular opinion. Most people (and religions) revere Jesus as a great man with teachings generally good for mankind, but they reject the belief that He was God in the flesh, who died on the cross and rose from the dead, and that he invites us to follow Him into His eternal kingdom.

I wrote my first book, "What If It's All True?" because of the apathy I see all around me. People may believe Jesus is the Son of God, but that belief isn't fueling their thoughts, words or actions very much. The people who met Jesus when he was here seemed to have one of two reactions to Him. Either they exclaimed: *Lord, to whom shall we go? You have the words of eternal life. We have come to believe and to know that you are the Holy One of God* (John 6:68-69)! Or, they feared their comfortable lives were so threatened by Jesus that they sought to kill Him. But no one was ambivalent about Jesus. Today, sadly, ambivalence abounds.

If we believe Jesus is who He claimed to be – the promised Messiah with supreme authority over the earth and all mankind – then there are infinite blessings for us who follow Him obediently. Moreover, because His Word is true, there are both temporal and eternal consequences for those who minimize His true being. It is healthy to periodically examine ourselves to see where we are growing in Christ, and where unnoticed slippage may have occurred. Pondering these thoughts as I write this feels good for my soul.

A wonderful pastor friend, Mike Minter, often spoke of the need for believers to grow in moral discernment. He would illustrate this by having three people come stand in front of the church. The person on one end of the line would represent God, and the one at the other end would represent culture. The person in between these two represented believers in Jesus. Then, Mike would slide the person portraying culture further away from God since culture is trending that direction. Then he would move the believer the same number of steps further from God showing them to be perhaps one step removed from culture but still moving ever further from what the Lord desires.

Moral discernment allows us to see life less from a human perspective and more through the eyes of Christ. His standard should be our only standard; not some compromised version. Churches right and left are changing their doctrines to appear more culturally relevant. Doctrinal deconstruction allows for people to keep what they like about their religion, but write off the difficult parts as being no longer relevant today – at least not for them.

In contrast to this, the Bible says *Jesus Christ is the same yesterday and today and forever* (Hebrews 13:8), and that *His word is eternal; it stands firm in the heavens* (Psalm 119:89).

Because it's all true, thriving is only found when we abide in His presence.

He is the light of the world and plenty capable to beckon his wayward children home. His doctrines have not changed, nor have his standards. His promises are true and He yearns for each of us to thrive in life. Because it's all true, thriving is only found when we abide in His presence.

I recently read Eric Mason's book, "Woke Church." Eric is an African-American pastor with a wise and scripture-laced view of the racial tension in America. He notes that, due to their dire circumstances, early pioneers of the black church developed a comprehensive theology that put the gospel in the center of every aspect of daily life. Life could not work unless Jesus was central to their family, work, community relationships, self-image, and so on.

Paul speaks often on this theme of the centrality of our relationship with Jesus: *May God himself, the God of peace, sanctify you through and through. May your whole spirit, soul and body be kept blameless at the coming of our Lord Jesus Christ* (1 Thessalonians 5:23).

In this journey with the Savior, we will experience thrills, spills, victories, and defeats. BUT, Jesus promises to be by our side throughout. The challenge is for us to recognize His presence so we enjoy Him in every facet of our lives.

John Stott taught that to be in Christ is to enjoy a vibrant, vital, organic relationship with Him, so that His life flows into us and we share His very life. This is a relationship characterized by faith, love, worship, and obedience. We cannot possibly claim to be mature disciples if we are living in disbelief or regular disobedience. Mature disciples are so closely related to Jesus Christ that they trust His promises, obey His commands, and fall down and worship Him acknowledging He is Lord.

What are signs that Jesus truly is in the center of our lives? See what you might add to these four:

1. Fruit of the Spirit (Galatians 5:22-23) – *When they saw the courage of Peter and John and realized that they were unschooled, ordinary men, they were astonished and they took note that these men had been with Jesus* (Acts 4:13). Do those around us take note that we have been with Jesus? Our character should reflect His character.

2. Engaged in Christian Community; the Church – *And God placed all things under His* [Jesus'] *feet and appointed Him to be head over everything for the church, which is His body, the fullness of Him who fills everything in every way* (Ephesians 1:22-23). Americans today are starved for authentic community. Our busy schedules and the false allure that social media builds community have left us wanting. Jesus offers his followers a place where they are accepted for who they are, both good and not so good. The Church is a place to come live, grow, and to thrive.

The Church has been a pillar for good news in communities the world over. The body of Christ has built countless hospitals, clinics, schools, orphanages, and established ministries committed to the mental, physical and social health of community members – not just believers in Christ but all people. *Instead, speaking the truth in love, we will grow to become in every respect the mature body of Him who is the head, that is, Christ. From Him the whole body, joined and held together by every supporting ligament, grows and builds itself up in love, as each part does its work* (Eph 4:15-16).

*(for more, see chapter 13, Our Call to the Church)

3. We are Drawn to Serve – *Even the Son of Man did not come to be served, but to serve, and give His life as a ransom for many* (Mark 10:45). Jesus gives His followers a heart for service. That's why we feel so good after doing something nice for someone else.

4. Mission – Followers of Jesus are called to a higher perspective, a Kingdom perspective. We aren't living primarily for this world but for our eternal home in Heaven. God wants all of His children to be with

Him there, but sin provides a barrier to the fulfillment of this vision. That is why Christians band together to share their faith with those who are lost in sin. We share not to be condemning, but to invite others to experience a love beyond anything in this world. We carry the words of eternal life. Jesus invites us to *Come, follow Me, and I will make you fishers of men* (Matthew 4:19). What a privilege!

Questions to Consider

1. What will it look like for you to be All IN with Jesus this year?

2. Are you expectantly participating in your sanctification? What does this look like to you?

3. Do those around you take note that you have been with Jesus? Do they note that your character reflects His character? Which Fruit of the Spirit from Galatians 5 would you like to focus on growing in this year? Note this in My Plan for Thriving.

4. Ask God to reveal any idols that receive more of your allegiance and time than Jesus. How can you reorder this imbalance?

CHAPTER 4

Connect with the Lord Deeply and Personally Part 1: God's Word

For the Word of God is alive and active. Sharper than any double-edged sword, it penetrates even to dividing soul and spirit, joints and marrow; it judges the thoughts and attitudes of the heart.
Hebrews 4:12

Thy Word is a lamp unto my feet, and a light unto my path.
Psalm 119:105

The Apostle John tells us that Jesus is the living Word of God – *The Word became flesh and made his dwelling among us. We have seen his glory, the glory of the one and only Son, who came from the Father, full of grace and truth* (John 1:14). When we observe Jesus in the gospels we get to know His character, His personality, His priorities and His mission. And because He is the living Word of God, we are then able to actually meet with Him when we read the Scriptures. For the believer, the Bible is no longer simply an historical writing – it is the present voice of God speaking to His people.

When I was introduced to a personal relationship with Jesus in high school, my Young Life leader, Marty, taught me the privilege of a Quiet Time; a time allotted to Bible reading and prayer with the goal to meet with Jesus and learn from Him. I made a habit of beginning my days sitting with the Lord, Bible in hand and prayer page in front of me, and it has continued to be the highlight of each day!

When a Christ-follower reads the Word of God, our Spirit interprets it to make it relevant for our needs. The Holy Spirit brings to mind thoughts for how to apply what we read. *Don't you know that you yourselves are God's temple and that God's Spirit dwells in your midst* (1 Corinthians 3:16)? These private sessions with the Lord lead to spiritual growth. As we seek to put God's Word into practice we begin to think, say, and do the things we see our Savior doing. Sanctification results.

Jesus reminded His disciples that, *I am the vine; you are the branches. If you remain in me and I in you, you will bear much fruit; apart from me you can do nothing* (John 15:5). That is why we in Young Life "pay" our staff to spend the first hour of each day in Bible study and prayer, communing intimately with the Savior. Apart from His work in our lives, we have nothing of substance to offer those to whom we minister. Hudson Taylor, the great missionary to inland China, shared this piece of wisdom: "Do you have your concert first, and then tune your instrument afterwards? Begin the day with the Word of God and prayer, and get first of all into harmony with Him."[4]

Tom Raley was one of the early pioneers of Young Life and a hero to many of us. One summer he served as the chaplain at our new staff training school. There, I heard him lead a seminar on the value of the quiet time and how to get the most from it. Not intending to brag, he casually mentioned that he had not missed beginning a day with the Lord in fifty-three years! THAT'S FIFTY-THREE YEARS!!! And the fruit of this compounded daily investment was evident in his Christ-like character. We were all inspired to mine the nuggets of wisdom available to us who diligently seek Jesus in the Scriptures.

Would you like greater wisdom, discernment and assurance in your life? (please don't say No!)

If you could sit down and have an intimate conversation with anyone who has ever lived, who would you choose? An ex-president? A hall of fame athlete? A master artist? Mother Theresa? And, if your chosen hero offered to meet with you as a personal coach each morning, would you adjust your busy schedule to take them up on their offer? Incredibly, this is what the Creator of the Universe, the Author and Perfecter of our Faith, the One who assigns purpose and meaning to our lives, made available to us when Jesus tore down the wall separating us from God. *Here I am! I stand at the door and knock. If anyone hears My voice and opens the door, I will come in and eat with that person, and they with Me* (Revelation 3:20).

Consider the benefits afforded us by the Lord's gracious invitation. We experience a personal touch of His love – not just for all mankind, but for us individually. We are assured of His forgiveness and favor. We glean from His eternal perspective. We gain vision, wisdom and discernment for the activities before us. And, we connect with His heart in prayer as we intercede for those in our sphere of influence. Why would we ever miss such a privileged encounter? Psalm One assures us of this: *Blessed is the man whose delight is in the Law of the Lord, and on His Law he meditates day and night. He is like a tree planted by streams of water, which yields its fruit in season and whose leaf does not wither. Whatever he does prospers.* This sounds a lot like thriving to me!

I recently heard an interesting insight into the encounter Moses had with God at the burning bush (Exodus 3:1-4). Moses decided to pay attention to this unusual occurrence – He turned aside to see, and by so doing, determined to explore what it might hold for his life. It was in response to Moses' initiative to turn toward God that the Lord spoke to him, *as a man speaks with a friend* (Exodus 33:11). What might "turning aside" to hear from the Lord look like for you? One response is to give Jesus the priority of the first meeting of the day.

Listen to these passages that communicate the Lord's desire to meet with you…

- *Call to Me and I will answer you, and show you great and unsearchable things you do not know* (Jeremiah 33:3).

- *And surely I am with you always, to the very end of the age* (Matthew 28:20).

- *But seek first his kingdom and his righteousness, and all these things will be given to you as well* (Matthew 6:33).

- *But when you pray, go into your room, close the door and pray to your Father, who is unseen. Then your Father, who sees what is done in secret, will reward you* (Matthew 6:6).

- *Ask and it will be given to you; seek and you will find; knock and the door will be opened to you. For everyone who asks receives; the one who seeks finds; and to the one who knocks, the door will be opened* (Matthew 7:7-8).

- *If you remain in me and my words remain in you, ask whatever you wish, and it will be done for you* (John 15:7).

Jesus modeled His own need for regular solitude with His Father.

Here are two pictures the Scriptures afford us: *Very early in the morning, while it was still dark, Jesus got up, left the house and went off to a solitary place, where he prayed* (Mark 1:35). Do you think He may have been tired from the rigors of His schedule? Do you think He could have used some extra time in the morning to prepare for His day, or maybe just read a book to relax? Sure! But He knew that NOTHING was as important as spending time with His Father, and the insights He might glean for the myriad of encounters the day would hold. Should that not be true of us?

The second picture comes from Jesus' temptation in the wilderness. When tempted by the devil for forty days, Jesus relied on God's Word to focus, strengthen, and assure Him so that He did not succumb – *Man shall not live on bread alone, but on every word that comes from the mouth of God* (Matthew 4:4).

We spend time with Jesus because we love Him; not because we fear Him.

The best way to live obediently, and to rise above the temptations all around us, is to draw strength from the Author of Life on a daily basis.

Know this: God did not send Jesus to bring forth moral compliance. Obedience that flows from a surrendered heart, full of love and gratitude, yields transformation from the inside out. It is joy-filled rather than dutiful. *We spend time with Jesus because we love Him; not because we fear Him.* My mentor, Chuck Reinhold, often reminded me that there is nothing you can do to cause God to love you any more or any less. Sitting quietly with the Lord doesn't earn the Lord's favor – He is already pleased with us!

In Colossians 1:18, Paul reminds us that, *He* (Jesus) *is the head of the body, the church, who is the beginning, the firstborn from the dead, that in all things He may have the preem-*

inence. Why not affirm our surrender to Jesus by giving Him the first meeting of each day? Consider these common reasons why folks struggle to give the Lord the first meeting of the day:

> "I'm not a morning person"
>
> "If I don't exercise in the morning I won't get to it"
>
> "I'm on kid duty in the morning"
>
> "I have to leave for school or work too early and need my sleep"
>
> "I feel like I'm just checking the box, not actually meeting with Jesus"
>
> "I don't think about what I read during my quiet time the rest of the day so why bother?"

Which one of these excuses trumps the rationale just laid out? What substitute for meeting with the Lord offers you more peace, direction, purpose, and guidance for your day? Which offers you keen insights for your significant relationships? And, which will benefit those in your circle of influence more than connecting with the Lord in the Scriptures and in prayer?

All that aside, I am not trying to make a legalistic case that we all must have morning quiet times. Some of those reasons mentioned, at least for a season, are certainly valid. The hope is you can carve out space somewhere in your day for this precious appointment.

The Key to a Life of Flourishing

In John 15, we find Jesus with His disciples in a vineyard just hours before His arrest and crucifixion. He used the image of grape vines and branches to hammer home the key to a thriving life, or as He phrased it, bearing much and lasting fruit. What was this key?

Eleven times in seventeen verses, Jesus used the word "abide," which means to stay with continually; to make one's home. *As the branch cannot bear fruit of itself, unless it abides in the vine, neither can you, unless you abide in Me* (John 15:4). Everything in the grapevine flows naturally to the branches. The riches of the Lord are at our disposal as we abide in Him.

I personally am not a big fan of devotional books where a respected author has you read a text and then tells you what they think it means. While there is a place for this sort of instruction, it does not teach us to engage the Scriptures for ourselves and to let the Holy Spirit speak to us based on our need at the moment. I prefer offering good, open-ended questions that the reader must answer for themselves. This helps equip us to stand alone in Christ since there may not always be someone else feeding us.

Here is a sampling of Bible study methods you might consider. Keeping a journal helps us remember key verses or applications, and it creates a list of themes to which we can refer back.

I. The Coe Method for Studying any Gospel Passage (easier)

1) What did Jesus think or feel?

2) What did Jesus say?

3) What did Jesus do?

*Now, as a follower of Jesus, write down what you will think, feel, say or do today to be more like Him.

II. Questions to ask about any passage in the new or old testaments (moderate)

1) What do I learn about God's character?

2) What do I learn about myself (or mankind)?

3) Where did I see Jesus? (He is at work in the Old Testament too!)

4) What can I do this week to grow in God's character?

III. The 3-Step Inductive Method (more advanced)

In order to read the Bible with understanding, we need to answer three primary questions:

1) What does the Bible say? (Observation)

2) What does the Bible mean? (Interpretation)

3) What does the Bible mean to me? (Application)

Step One: Observation

1) Who – Who is the author of the book? To what specific audience are they writing? Who are the major and minor characters of the book?

2) What – What events are taking place? What words or ideas are repeated or are central to the passage?

3) When – Are there any references to the time, day, month or year or to when events took place in relation to other events?

4) Where – Where do the events occur? Are there references to towns, cities, provinces? If so, look these up on a Bible map.

Step Two: Interpretation

1) Were there any words you didn't understand? Look them up.

2) Were major ideas presented? Try to grasp their meaning and significance.

3) How – How is the passage written? Is it a letter, speech, poem, parable? Does the author use any figures of speech (similes, metaphors, parables)? Why do you suppose he chose this style?

4) Why – What do you suppose was the author's purpose in writing this passage?

Step Three: Application

Rule # 1: Whenever our situation corresponds to that faced by the original readers, God's word to us is the same as it was to them.

Rule # 2: Whenever our situation does not correspond to that faced by the original readers, we should look for the principle(s) underlying God's Word to them. We can then apply that principle to comparable situations in our own lives.

Once you understand these principles, you can ask…

- Is there a command for me to obey?
- Is there a promise to claim?
- Is there an example to follow?
- Is there a sin to avoid or confess?
- Is there a reason for thanksgiving or praise?
- What does this passage teach me about God, Jesus, the Holy Spirit, myself, others?

IV. Bridge Method – building a bridge between the world of the Bible and our world.

1) What did this Scripture mean when it was written?

2) What is the timeless truth behind what God is saying?

3) How does it apply now to me?

V. Swedish Method (a symbol denotes each question)

1) Light bulb –What stuck out to you?

2) Question mark –What questions did this passage raise?

3) Cross – Where did you see Jesus in this passage?

4) Arrow – What is an application for my life today?

5) Talking bubble – How might I share the joy, peace, conviction or truth given by God with others?

6) Exclamation point – What is the author's main point?

Experiment with a few of these methods and find a style that works for you. Be careful to change things up periodically so as not to get stuck in a rut. All God's best!

Questions to Consider

1. Do you have trouble feeling like Jesus is with you when you read the Bible? If so, why do you suspect that is?

2. What is the chief obstacle keeping you from a regular daily quiet time? Do you see a remedy?

3. Which of the suggested Bible study methods sounds inviting to try? Why? Is there someone you would like to encourage or hold you accountable to your commitment to spending time in God's Word? Note this in My Plan for Thriving.

CHAPTER 5

Connect with the Lord Deeply and Personally
Part 2: Prayer

The prayer of a righteous person is
powerful and effective.
James 5:16b

If you remain in Me and My words remain in you,
ask whatever you wish,
and it will be done for you.
John 15:7

As for me, far be it from me that I should sin
against the Lord by failing to pray for you. And I
will teach you the way that is good and right.
1 Samuel 12:23

One of the absolute joys of my morning routine is lifting up my friends, Young Life alumni, family and neighbors before the Lord in prayer. I have carved out about 400 names that are divided over six days. When I pray for each day's list I recall fond memories of our times together, and I ask the Lord to continue moving each one ever closer to Himself. I also pray for the impact of their faith upon those in their circles of influence.

A number of years ago I read the verse above (1 Samuel 12:23) and asked the Lord who He expected me to be praying for, so much so that it would be a sin if I neglected to do so. That led me to expand my list to include some people that perhaps no one else is praying for since they have been entrusted to my responsibility.

Have you asked the Lord who He is counting on you to be praying for? There is no greater force for change in all the world – no medicine, no political hero, nothing will bring righteousness like our humble petitions.

Prayer is like a conversation with the Lord that goes both directions. Jesus desires to hear our praises, our thanksgivings, our confessions and our petitions. He desires to speak to us as a man speaks with a friend (Exodus 33:11). Learning to listen for the sound of His voice through the Spirit is quite a challenge (see chapter 20 for great ideas!). Jesus promises that if we Seek first His kingdom and His righteousness, all these things will be given us as well. Jesus will honor our seeking of greater intimacy with Him; trust me!

Different Prayers for Different Purposes

There are many different kinds of prayers and they serve different purposes. As with the handling of God's Word, I recommend cross-training where we experiment with different ways of praying so as to continue growing our "prayer muscles" in fresh ways.

The A-C-T-S (ACTS method) is a tried and true model that can serve as a baseline for whatever prayer strategy you formulate for yourself:

> A = Adoration – God desires our praise and it feeds our soul as we remind ourselves of his

goodness and the many qualities of his nature. Praying some of the psalms back to God is an example of adoration. This is a great way to begin a time of prayer.

C = Confession – Trying to run through life with unconfessed sin is like running with shackles on our ankles. Jesus paid an amazing price so we might be relieved from the weight of sin and free to thrive in an intimate relationship with Him. John the Apostle assures us that *If we confess our sins, he is faithful and just and will forgive us our sins and purify us from all unrighteousness* (1 John 1:9). What a gift!

T = Thanksgiving (not the holiday!) – Taking time to thank God for all He has done and is doing for us reminds us of some of our core beliefs and fuels our sanctification. The parable of the healing of ten lepers reminds us that Jesus likes to be thanked for answered prayers and his goodness to us (Luke 17:11-19).

S = Supplication – These are the requests and intercessions we bring to the feet of Almighty God.

For those a bit more advanced, Lectio Divina is another way to connect with the Lord in prayer. Instead of studying the Bible with pen in hand looking for applications, the goal is to read Scripture until we come into the presence of God then rest there. Have no other agenda but to enjoy His presence with you. It can help to read the same small passage a few times over and plunge deeper into the Lord's arms as you go.

Principles to Guide our Prayers

Scripture gives us some principles for efficacy in prayer we should keep in mind…

1. We are instructed to pray with faith, believing and picturing our prayers as answered (Matthew 21:22)

2. Pray in Jesus' Name (John 16:24, Ephesians 5:20) as there is unlimited power there.

3. Pray in His will (1 John 5:14, Luke 22:42). Often, unanswered prayers are those not in keeping with God's will.

4. Pray continually (1 Thessalonians 5:17). We shouldn't only pray on our prayer carpet, but as we walk, workout, drive the car, work, etc. (see chapter 8 – the Lord is interested in every aspect of our lives!)

5. Pray with a grateful heart – give thanks in all circumstances (Psalm 100:4, Colossians 3:15)

6. Pray with our sins confessed (James 5:16)

7. Pray with a humble posture (Psalm 34:18, Lk 18:14)

Who Should be Included in our Prayers

I believe there should be at least one time of prayer each day that is strategic and organized, not just a time to lift up whomever or whatever comes to mind. 1 Samuel 12:23 urges us to steward in prayer all within our circle of influence. Here are just a few people and priorities to pray for that Scripture asks us to prioritize in our prayer strategies:

1. Our political leaders, president, and all in authority (1 Timothy 2:1-3)

2. Pastors and spiritual leaders (Ephesians 6:19-20, Colossians 4:3)

3. Our families, extended and nuclear

4. Those who are sick (James 5:14-15)

5. Our inner circle of Christian friends (Galatians 6:9-10)

6. Our enemies (Matthew 5:44; Acts 7:59-60)

7. Israel, God's covenant people (Psalm 122:6; Isaiah 62:6-7, Romans 10:1)

8. Our neighbors, friends and teachers who don't yet know the Lord (1 Timothy 2:1)

9. Peace in the world ((Luke 2:14, Leviticus 26:6)

10. Open doors for the gospel, and those who preach the gospel (Colossians 4:3; 2 Thessalonians 3:1-2)

11. God's Kingdom to come and His will to be done (Matthew 6:9-10)

12. Those who have come to faith through our ministry (that they keep growing!) (John 17:9)

13. Sin in the church (John 5:16)

14. Ourselves and our pertinent needs (Genesis 24:12; Matthew 14:30; Luke 23:42)

   a) Physical provision (Matthew 6:11)

   b) Deliverance from evil (Matthew 6:13)

   c) Forgiveness of those who have wronged us (Matthew 6:12-15)

Obviously, this list can feel overwhelming, and we certainly aren't expected to pray for all of these things each day. That is why building a manageable prayer strategy is an effective way to steward this wonderful privilege of access to the Lord.

Questions to Consider

1. Would you say your prayers currently are more strategic or free-flowing?

2. When you pray, are you able to picture God listening to you? Do you ever hear him reply (see chapter 20)?

3. With which types of praying are you most comfortable, and which ones are you less familiar?

4. With 1 Samuel 12:23 in mind, develop a responsible prayer strategy that includes the persons and priorities for which God asks us to pray, and the people in our inner circle of influence.

CHAPTER 6

Develop a Kingdom Perspective

Since, then, you have been raised with Christ,
set your hearts on things above, where Christ is,
seated at the right hand of God. Set your minds on
things above, not on earthly things. For you died,
and your life is now hidden with Christ in God.
Colossians 3:1–3

But seek first his kingdom and his righteousness,
and all these things will be given to you as well.
Matthew 6:33

A daily intake of God's Word serves as an algorithm to further fortify a Kingdom mindset for believers. The Apostle Peter compares a craving for the Word of God as a newborn craves milk. In other words, thoroughly digesting the Word of God is not optional but essential for our focus, our nurture, and our daily thriving. We have been reborn with a craving for God's Word, and a healthy intake of the Word helps form a Kingdom Perspective.

Everyone sees life through a certain lens. This lens, or perspective, is formed by our experiences and what we are taught by those we respect. We've all heard the terms "died in the wool Democrat or Republican," meaning one who has been raised with a political leaning in keeping with the party of their ancestors. Wealthy people might see life through a perspective of privilege, whereas a poor immigrant may see life as a struggle with little hope of overcoming poverty. These lenses not only can distort, but also limit both our reality and what is possible. Albert Mohler wisely teaches that, "One of the cardinal principles of the Biblical worldview is that all issues interconnect."[5]

My sweet wife, Kris, recently developed cataracts. They cause her vision to be blurred a bit (so why is she still driving!). If left untreated, clouding of the eye lens will worsen as less light is permitted to penetrate. Just as we desire clear vision to navigate, we also need spiritually clear vision to discern the path God is laying out for us. Jesus said, *The eye is the lamp of the body. If your eyes are healthy, your whole body will be full of light* (Matthew 6:22).

Nothing can change our perspective more than becoming a new creation in Christ (2 Corinthians 5:17). Jesus told Nicodemus the Pharisee that one must be born again if they want to see the Kingdom of God. If we want to see what God sees, we must surrender to Jesus and invite His Spirit to direct our thinking, our speech, our goals, and our vision for life.

So we fix our eyes not on what is seen, but on what is unseen, since what is seen is temporary, but what is unseen is eternal (2 Corinthians 4:18). The lens through which we see life is so important. The following chart contrasts the two perspectives competing for our allegiance.

Human Perspective	Kingdom Perspective
Love, when loved first	Love, not conditional on response
Happiness, when circumstances are good	Joy, regardless of circumstances
Stress due to the need to control circumstances	Peace, due to trusting circumstances are controlled by God
Impatient due to a critical view of others	Patient because we view others as broken
Self-centered, me first	Kind, others first
Sinful, prone to do what we want	Righteous, prone to do what God wants
Harsh	Gentle, we touch others with grace
Volatile, unprincipled	Self-controlled, disciplined and consistent
Self-confident	Humble, reminded of who's in control

You were taught, with regard to your former way of life, to put off your old self, which is being corrupted by its deceitful desires; to be made new in the attitude of your minds; and to put on the new self, created to be like God in true righteousness and holiness (Ephesians 4:22-24).

Perspective for Handling Painful Moments in Life from my friend, pastor Pat Goodman

Life has its share of great elation and tremendous disappointment. One minute you can feel like you're on top of the world, only to quickly be side swiped by heartache. Our task is to be able to embrace the richness of life, as well as confront its challenges, from the same foundation. It's easy to tie our well-being to the tide of our circumstances pulling at us in all directions. But what if we could learn a way for our soul to "stay at rest" regardless of what life offers? A way that enables us to fully enjoy what is good, while not denying what is hard. A way to live that isn't enslaved to a fear of loss or pain, but one that enables us to face life honestly and courageously whatever happens.

In the book of Daniel, we find Daniel, Shadrach, Meshach, and Abednego having experienced God's favor before king Nebuchadnezzar. God gave them supernatural knowledge. Daniel was also given the capacity to interpret the King's dream causing Nebuchadnezzar to declare, '*Surely your God is the God of gods and the Lord of kings, and revealer of mysteries...*' (Daniel 2:47). Daniel and his three friends were appointed to be administrators over the province of Babylon. Life seemed to be humming along – that is until it wasn't!

As much as Nebuchadnezzar admired Daniel's God, he admired the 90-foot golden image he had crafted even more. So much so that he made a declaration that if anyone doesn't bow down and worship this statue they would be thrown into a blazing furnace. This put Shadrach, Meshach, and Abednego in a tough place because they knew who was worthy of their worship and they refused to budge; they had a Kingdom perspective. *O Nebuchadnezzar, we do not need to defend ourselves before you in this matter. If we are thrown into the blazing furnace, the God we serve is able to save us from it, and he will rescue us from your hand. But even if He does not, we want you to know, O King, that we will not serve your gods or worship the image of gold you have set up* (Daniel 3:16-18).

God is able, but not obligated to rescue us from hard things. He is worthy of our trust no matter what happens.

Potential pain and suffering can make taking short cuts to maintain comfort feel completely reasonable. Being thrown into a furnace would qualify as something to avoid. But there is a more pressing issue to face besides trying to avoid things in life that are difficult – it is knowing there is someone we can trust who has both our well-being in mind, and the power to make sure things work out in the end.

Here are a few building blocks for a Kingdom Perspective we can glean from Shadrach, Meshach, and Abednego:

1. Their response to the King was a team effort. They drew strength from one another's faith and stood together as they stared a potentially painful death in the face. We need each other in hard times. Presence far exceeds words when it comes to giving strength and empowering our mutual faith. We need the Church!

2. God is able, but not obligated to rescue us from hard things. He is worthy of our trust no matter what happens.

3. God's faithfulness in the past, when things worked out as we had hoped, is no different from who He is in the present if things don't work out as we desire. Who He is doesn't change.

4. They didn't allow their circumstances to form their view of God or alter their response to potential pain. Our level of comfort isn't the defining factor for the Lord's worthiness to be trusted.

5. Our response to pain and suffering is a witness to others about the God we worship.

6. They had already decided to "give up" their lives to the Living God – so in essence whatever life brought their way was seen through that lens. Luke 9:23 reminds us that when we commit to follow Jesus we must die to ourselves.

7. The Lord shows up in ways we'd never imagine in the "fires" of life to bring relief and comfort.

It's powerful to think that these three heroes agreed the Lord "would rescue them," but "even if He doesn't" they would remain faithful. They were certain God would rescue them one way or another. For them, dying in the fire was better than denying the God they loved and trusted.

Once we decide we are sticking with God regardless of what life throws at us, inner peace is possible. I (Pat) experienced this over 20 years ago when our daughter Jessica almost died. The ICU doctor told my wife and me that she was the sickest person in the hospital and if anyone was likely to die within the next 24 hours it would be her due to an infection that was impacting her lungs. I remember staring out the hallway window at the hospital watching a beautiful sunrise, while I could see our daughter on a ventilator a short distance away. I felt the paradox of creation screaming to me of God's power, creativity, beauty, and provision. I also knew our daughter's life was hanging in the balance. I knew God was able to heal her, but the real question for me was what would I do if He didn't? This was a gut check to my Kingdom perspective.

What was readily clear to me was that I couldn't wait to see how things turned out before I decided if the Lord was who I thought He was and worthy of my trust. Through tears staring out at a magnificent sunrise I uttered the words "I'm trusting you Lord no matter what – give me strength." In that moment I felt the Lord gently pose this question: "Before Jessica was even conceived, if you knew you'd only share 18 years of life with her this side of glory, would you have wanted it?" In my heart I said, "Yes 100 out of 100 times!"

I realized I had subtly treated my daughter, a gift God had graciously given us, as a possession, and I did not want Him to take her back. Fortunately, Jessica recovered. But I learned that God is able even if she hadn't.

When life is good, God seems good. But when life is painful God seems to be anything but good. As Donald McCullough said in his book, *The Trivialization of God*, "….we often end up worshipping a god of our own imagination, desires, expectations, wants, dreams, etc, but not the One True God who is worthy of our trust no matter what."

When we see life through Kingdom eyes we are blessed to participate in eternal activity. We grow in wisdom, in fruitfulness, and enjoy the fulfillment that comes from thriving in Christ.

Questions to Consider

1. How do we go about putting on a Kingdom perspective? What can you do to grow in this process?

2. Are there certain types of situations that make it difficult for you to see and act from a Kingdom perspective?

3. What fruit from operating from a Kingdom perspective have you experienced? What steps might you add to My Plan for Thriving to make these experiences more normative?

CHAPTER 7

Know Your Purpose and Calling

But you are a chosen people, a royal priesthood, a holy nation, God's special possession, that you may declare the praises of Him who called you out of darkness into his wonderful light.
1 Peter 2:9

Many are the plans in a person's heart, but it is the LORD's purpose that prevails.
Proverbs 19:21

But the plans of the LORD stand firm forever, the purposes of his heart through all generations.
Psalms 33:1

The Purpose of All Mankind

Our purpose in life gives meaning to our existence. When we don't know who we are or why we are here we open the door to unnecessary anxiety and depression. We fall prey to the illusion that our lives are of no real significance. This breaks the Lord's heart!

A key building block to a life of thriving is knowing our purpose in life. Surveys confirm that most people believe their lives have a purpose, but, according to a 2018 NY Times study, only 25% of Americans say they know what that purpose is.[6] That means 75% are left wandering aimlessly without even a picture of what it is they seek, or what can make their lives feel truly meaningful.

Once a lawyer asked Jesus, "*What is the greatest commandment in the Law?*" In other words, he was asking Jesus what one thing would be worthy of his entire focus; his very purpose for living. Jesus replied: "*Love the Lord your God with all your heart and with all your soul and with all your mind. This is the first and greatest commandment. And the second is like it: Love your neighbor as yourself. All the Law and the Prophets hang on these two commandments* (Matthew 22:34-40)."

Simply put, our purpose is to love God and love people. Loving God means trusting His ways are good and committing to do what He says. And, loving our, neighbor as ourselves is the remedy for all crime, war, theft, and general misconduct in the world. We work together for the thriving of everyone! Every day on the news we hear talking heads pose remedies for all the upheaval taking place in society – less guns to cut down on senseless murders, more police to curb violence on subways, more mental health workers to address suicide with teens – and the list goes on. Of course these suggestions can be of some help, but in the long run they are only band aids that don't actually fix the gaping wound. The only way people who sin will change is by a change of heart.

Simplyput, ourpurpose is to love God and love people.

Jesus said, *The good person out of the good treasure of his heart produces good, and the evil person out of his evil treasure produces evil, for out of the abundance of the heart his mouth speaks* (Luke 6:45). Our actions are motivated by who owns our heart. The only way there will be moral reform in our country is if there is a spiritual revival and multitudes of people have a heart change. Because it's all true, following Jesus and living as He directs is the best investment we can make in our world.

It would be difficult to put too much stock in a purpose we invent ourselves. Most likely it would be hit or miss with frequent changes based on what we are experiencing at the time. To be confident in our purpose requires a belief that this purpose is assigned by one with authority – someone greater than us.

Why Purpose Eludes So Many

Until quite recently most Americans believed in the triune God as the source of absolute truth. We know for a fact that gravity exists and that triangles aren't squares. We can jump off a building if we want but choosing not to believe in gravity won't keep us from falling. It is clear to any rational mind that there are in fact truths which are absolute. Despite this, many people today work hard to convince themselves that truth is something we are each free to invent.

Consider just a small sampling of how invented truths are impacting our culture:

- Squatters are allowed to remain in houses they illegally claim a rite to but do not own.

- Looters are free to steal from businesses without prosecution because their truth is that they are owed things for free.

- Young kids and teens are free to believe they are a gender other than what was assigned them by God at birth.

- We can have a sovereign nation without enforced borders or a plan for immigration.

Our Unique Individual Purpose

In Ephesians 4, Paul exhorts this young church to: *...live a life worthy of the calling you have received.* But what is that calling? Is it the same for all of us, or does it change from person to person? A thorough reading of the Scriptures depicts our purpose similar to a funnel. There are some universal directives true for all mankind at the top of the funnel. Then, as the funnel descends and narrows, some more specific callings are revealed for each individual to discern.

At the top of the funnel is the Great Command we just discussed from Matthew 22 – to love God and love people. The next layer of the funnel is the Great Commission which is our universal calling to: *Go into all the world and proclaim the gospel to the whole creation* (Mark 16:15). These universal truths give purpose to every individual God has made. But then the funnel begins to narrow and our purpose becomes more individualized.

An example of a more personal calling is evidenced in Acts 13:2 – *While they were worshiping the Lord and fasting, the Holy Spirit said, 'Set apart for me Barnabas and Saul for the work to which I have called them.'* The Spirit spoke of things He had in store uniquely for Barnabas and Saul. Similarly, the book of Romans lists various gifts given to people according to His plan or calling for them – *For just as each of us has one body with many members, and these members do not all have the same function, so in Christ we, though many, form one body, and each member belongs to all the others. We have different gifts, according to the grace given to each of us. If your gift is prophesying, then prophesy in accordance with your faith; if it is serving, then serve; if it is teaching, then teach; if it is to encourage, then give encouragement; if it is giving, then give generously; if it is to lead, do it diligently; if it is to show mercy, do it cheerfully* (Romans 12:4-8). If we have received the Lord, we know we have been gifted for meaningful service.

Pastor Tony Evans believes, "You have not really lived until you have found your God-given ministry. To live without a sense of divine appointment is to simply exist, to be detached from an eternal perspective and, therefore simply marking time."[7]

Most of our experiences in life were given to us for a reason. They teach us what we like and don't like. They show us where we excel and where we struggle. Recording some key themes from our life's experiences helps us discern what our unique calling is within the body of Christ.

(See Appendix 4 for developing your personal mission statement.)

'For I know the plans I have for you,' declares the Lord, 'plans to prosper you and not to harm you, plans to give you hope and a future. Then you will call on Me and come and pray to Me, and I will listen to you. You will seek Me and find Me when you seek Me with all your heart' (Jeremiah 29:11-13).

Questions to Consider

1. Before reading this chapter, were you confident you knew your purpose in life? How about now?

2. How does knowing your life's purpose impact how you invest your time, money, and prayers?

3. Do you know your unique gifts and calling? How do you feel about them, and how are they being deployed? Perhaps note in My Plan for Thriving how you intend to invest in the further development of your gifts.

CHAPTER 8

Live a Fully-Integrated Life – Christ Is Interested in Every Part of Us!

Therefore keep the words of this covenant and
do them, that you may prosper in all that you do.
Deuteronomy 29:9

In all your ways acknowledge him,
and he will make straight your paths.
Proverbs 3:6

All things were created through Him and for Him. And He is before all things, and in Him all things hold together. And He is the head of the body, the church. He is the beginning, the firstborn from the dead, that in everything He might be preeminent.
Colossians 1:16b-18

On a scale of 1-10, with 1 being none at all, and 10 being everything, how much of your life do you think Jesus is interested in? Do you really think He cares if He is part of your family life, hobbies, work, friendships, your personal goals, or even your sporting events? I mean does He really care about your golf score or favorite cake recipe? In this chapter, I make the case that, YES, the Lord desires to be involved with you in every aspect of your life because He cares for your entire being. After all, you are an image bearer of the Lord!

Consider for a moment some of your weekly rhythms… how much do you look to Jesus to join you in them? If you're like me, the answer is far too little. The famous Hollywood Presbyterian Church Bible teacher, Henrietta Mears, taught, "If He is not Lord of all, He is not Lord at all."[8] Think about it, we who are in Christ have a new identity, we have been adopted into God's family and are fully His children. He didn't just adopt our head or left arm. He adopted our whole body, our whole mind, our gifts, talents, as well as our warts – all of it! Jesus died to redeem every bit of us.

Listen to this truth from King David: *The Lord directs the steps of the godly. He delights in every detail of their lives. Though they stumble, they will never fall, for the Lord holds them by the hand* (Psalm 37:23-24). Imagine what the fruit of our lives might be if we acknowledged Jesus as central in every detail of our lives.

Who gave us the abilities we uniquely possess? Since the Lord gifted us to excel in all our various interests, don't you think He is eager to be involved in them with us? David Bahnsen, founder of an investment strategy and wealth management company, wrote a book titled, "Full-Time: Work and the Meaning of Life." Reflecting on the Genesis statement that we humans were made in God's image, Bahnsen says: "We were the unique part of creation that was tasked with co-creating with Him, building with Him, taking the raw materials of the world and going about being fruitful, multiplying, filling the earth, cultivating the earth, and caring for the garden. There was a spirit of creativity and productivity that God Himself shared with us." In other words, "Our efforts in vocation, commerce, education, technology, and entrepreneurial endeavors are all things that have profound significance to God and are a by-product of what God created us for."[9]

In August of 2025, Pope Leo the 14th urged Catholic politicians to integrate their faith into every aspect of public service. He told a delegation of Bishops, "There is not on one side the politician, and on the other the Christian. Rather, there is the politician who, under the gaze of God and of his conscience, lives out his commitments and his responsibilities in a Christian manner."[10]

STEM programs are gaining popularity in education. They take the four disciplines of Science, Technology, Engineering, and Math and, instead of just focusing on each one separately, seeks to integrate all four. The result of this integration is a high degree of critical thinking, problem solving, and overall competency. Similarly, followers of Jesus who integrate their faith and make it central to every aspect of their lives experience joy and thriving. They stop feeling like they have different personas depending on who they are with or what they are doing.

John Mark Comer teaches that becoming a follower of Jesus requires a high bar of entry: "It will require you to reorder your entire life around following Jesus as your undisputed top priority, over your job, your money, your reputation – over everything. Yet all these things will find their rightful place once integrated into a life of apprenticeship."[11]

In chapter sixteen I discuss building a wall to overcome the onslaught of the devil's attacks. In the Chronicles of Narnia C.S. Lewis addresses the importance of fortifying ourselves with a fully-integrated faith. Lauren Meyers offers this synopsis from Lewis' work: "In a series of letters, Screwtape instructs his nephew, Wormwood, in the art of temptation. Screwtape targets human nature separating and distorting our soul and body. Neither the body nor the soul need to be destroyed outright; they merely need to be disassociated from one another. If the patient cannot integrate the body and soul, then they will never fully know them self or their Creator."[12]

The fruit of living a Christ-centered life is the potential for a consistent sense of joy and peace. When Jesus is invited into the core of our every activity we become one of those "glass half-full" people that light up a room. Regardless of the challenges we face, we know we will be OK because the Lord carries us in the palm of His hand. Because it's all true!

Questions to Consider

1. Did this chapter spark any new thoughts?

2. What parts of your life are easy to invite Jesus into, and which parts are either difficult or don't seem very natural?

3. What fruit could come from inviting Jesus into your highest priority spaces? Write a goal or action in My Plan for Thriving to help you succeed.

CHAPTER 9

Get on Mission!

But you will receive power when the Holy Spirit comes upon you. And you will be my witnesses in Jerusalem, and in all Judea and Samaria, and to the ends of the world.
Acts 1:8

Come, follow Me, and I will make you fishers of men.
Matthew 4:19

In the fall of my senior year of college I was involved in terrible car-totaling accident at highway speed. I found myself rolling on the ground in pain thinking I was going to die. I remember crying out to God, "Don't take me now, for I haven't been living as you would like." I was a fairly new believer and was living with a foot in both worlds; wanting to be true to my faith but also blend in with my surrounding culture. Spoiler alert: I survived!

The result of coming through that trial was that I decided to put Christ first in my life. So, I GOT ON MISSION. I started a Christian fellowship on campus, and began following a vision for the importance of not only living for Christ, but reaching out to those who don't know what they're missing. That accident was part of what led me to full-time ministry as a career.

T or F: It feels better to contribute to others than to take help from others? I think I know how the majority of you responded. Nearly every generation has sought to make the world better than they found it. Altruistic service to our community is highly prized. Look at the appreciation shown firefighters, police, the military, and first responders. They are difference-makers, and often pay a high price for the sake of those they serve.

Jesus bookended His mission with a charge to his followers to evangelize; to make an eternal difference by getting on mission. In one of His first sermons, Jesus told his disciples, *You are the light of the world. Let your light shine before others, that they may see your good deeds and glorify your Father in heaven* (Matthew 5:14,16). Then, in His final words prior to His ascension, Jesus commissioned his faithful team to go and make disciples of all nations. From His teachings in between, we can discern at least two motives for this call to mission.

First, the Lord's desire is to redeem the entire world, all His lost children, so He privileges us to be His hands and feet toward that ultimate objective. We've been chosen to be on God's team! Second, He wants us to walk in faith because He knows that we grow more when we're pushed out of our comfort zones and forced to depend on Him. It is scary sharing with others the hope we have in Christ, so we are forced to pray and lean on His Spirit for guidance. This draws us to utterly depend on Him.

We can't very well share the gospel unless we know the gospel, so the challenge to witness presses us to know Christ and our theology more fully. Theologian Hans Urs von Balthasar consistently taught that one doesn't know who they are until they discover their mission.[13] While every member of the body of Christ is called to the Great Commission, each individual member is assigned a specific role to play in this great struggle. We have been uniquely gifted, placed in community, and given experiences that fuel our mission. It is fair to say we actually "find ourselves" when we engage in our mission.

Once a young believer has seen their life make an eternal impact on someone else, they are hooked as few things will ever seem as significant. This certainly was my experience. A short time after my car accident, a college friend named Donny started asking me a barrage of questions about Christianity. He was a pre-med student and a much deeper thinker than me. I tried as best I could to answer him but I'm sure my responses were clumsy at best. Finally, out of the blue, Donny asked how he could give his life to Christ. We fumbled through a prayer together and I witnessed this friend become a child of God. I knew he was changed forever, and so was I!

I take no credit for introducing Donny to the Lord as it was all the Spirit's work. But being invited into that experience showed me what I wanted to be about during my time here on earth. I wanted to introduce people to a life-transforming relationship with Jesus and help them grow in their faith. Why settle for only temporal impact when eternal impact is at our finger tips? And we don't need to be in full-time ministry to be on mission. Living on mission is a mindset, not a job description.

Living on mission is a mindset, not a job description.

In Luke 10 Jesus sends out seventy-two disciples on a missionary journey to a number of small towns He soon planned to visit. They were told to depend fully on Him – not to take food, purse or extra sandals, but to depend on His provision to succeed. What a faith building time this must have been! Why did Jesus deploy this team? Is it because He needed their help to reach the people in these towns? Certainly not! Jesus could have done it himself, but He chose to send these friends because He knew that experience would radically grow their faith. Jesus loves to be trusted, and these men now trusted Him much more than before!

Pastor Michelle Jones is responsible for spiritual formation at Imago Dei in Portland. She teaches that, "Sharing the grace we have been given is not only evidence of our transformation; it is itself transforming. Every opportunity to share our faith challenges us to live out what we say we believe."[14]

Thankfully, the Young Life ministry in which I have been involved for four decades, has historically embraced a passion for reaching not only lost teens, but the furthest out kids. Our mission statement is: "Introducing adolescents to Jesus Christ and helping them grow in their faith." We are all about outreach; but, our mission statement reminds us that effective outreach only occurs when we disciple our converts and in turn invite them into this missional calling with us. That is why we challenge our Christian students (we call Campaigners) to step out in faith and invite their non-Christian friends to Young Life club. We want them to stick their necks out and be counted as one of Christ's own among their peers.

Just as the Lord delegates to us the responsibility to reach the world for Christ, we equip kids with the vision to reach their inner circle of friends. Even if the Young Life leaders could run dynamic ministries without Campaigners, we wouldn't, because it would deprive them of the opportunity to grow closer to Jesus as they put their faith on the line.

Witnessing is a multi-faceted gift from the Lord. I love the gospel story where the man for whom Jesus cast out a legion of demons begged Jesus to allow him to join his traveling band of disciples. Instead of granting this request for sweet fellowship and certain growth, Jesus tells him to *Return home and tell how much God has done for you* (Luke 8:39a). Jesus didn't need this man to do His work for Him; instead, He offered him this role because of how much it would grow his young faith. I wish the gospel writers had recorded the impact of this man's ministry as I suspect it was profound!

Seminaries have gotten a bad rap through the decades for training men and women with sound head knowledge but too little practical application. Jesus doesn't want fat little Christians (thank you Amy Grant!) who are content with fellowship alone – He wants world changers willing to sacrifice everything for the sake of establishing His Kingdom here on earth.

In closing, I submit that both Fellowship and Mission are essential for spiritual thriving. We benefit from the support of believers around us, by their instruction, and the full range of gifts the body of Christ offers. We are called to the Church.

We grow from mission by being forced out of our comfort zone to depend on the Lord. Mission teaches us to pray like we mean it! Mission teaches us how we are gifted so we know where we can contribute. We glean vision for Kingdom impact as we dream dreams well beyond our reach alone. Jesus said, *Do not work for food that spoils, but for food that endures to eternal life, which the Son of Man will give you* (John 6:27). As my mentor Chuck used to say, "This is living!"

We are God's Plan A for redeeming this lost world, and there is no Plan B. All of us are called to be ministers of the gospel. We are only here for a short time – let's be intentional and help one another to live ON MISSION!

Questions to Consider

1. Can you recall a time where God used you to help lead someone to Christ? If so, how did it feel? If not, why do you think you have yet to have such an experience?

2. What holds you back from witnessing more often? Would witnessing in tandem with another believer be of help?

3. Take a few minutes to record in My Plan for Thriving some steps you will take to grow in your proficiency as a witness to Jesus.

CHAPTER 10

Serve Others: Make the Golden Rule a Habit!

In everything, do to others what you would have them do to you, for this sums up the Law and the Prophets
Matthew 7:12

Do nothing from selfish ambition or empty conceit, but in humility regard others as better than yourselves. Let each of you look not to your own interests but to the interests of others.
Philippians 2:3-4

For even the Son of Man did not come to be served, but to serve, and to offer His life as a ransom for many.
Mark 10:45

The term "Servant," for many, brings to mind some negative images. Servants are a lowly class, and probably not in a stage of life they desire. Many servants feel like prisoners under the control of someone they did not choose. The ancient Israelites who heard Jesus say the words of Mark 10:45 above must have been flabbergasted. But let's look beyond the term servant and examine the benefits of serving.

A quality imbedded in our DNA is the desire to make a difference. There are many ways to have impact – through dynamic leadership, faithful labor in our job, setting an outstanding example, raising children of noble character, and the list goes on. But a proven means for making a difference is to enter into needs of our neighbors and offer both compassion and practical help. Serving others is a part of our calling, and a great investment in our spiritual life. Service gives our faith a workout, and it also gives the oft blemished church a favorable view.

An 85-year ongoing study conducted by Harvard Research evaluated the backgrounds of over 700 "high achievers" and found a strong correlation between doing household chores and later professional success.[15] Children who were tasked to do chores experienced greater success and happiness as they matured. There was also a strong correlation between doing chores (serving) and higher self-esteem. The kids who did chores arose to be more confident and competent than their peers whose parents solved all their problems for them. In short, kids become less self-centered when they join forces to share the workload. When we do everything for them and they don't have to participate, it creates the illusion the world revolves around them.

Ezra 7:10 says, *For Ezra had set his heart to study the Law of the LORD, and to do it and to teach his statutes and rules in Israel.* Too often believers take in great teaching that remains in their heads rather than getting traction with their feet. How many Sunday churchgoers can remember the point of yesterday's sermon come Monday noon? Almost none! Pete Roth, a dear friend and mentor, makes a practice of writing down at least one thing to do following his morning devotions. This keeps God's Word from that day imprinted in his mind and available for action.

Service gives application to what Jesus is teaching us. Information transmission has its place, but what we all deeply want is a faith that is integrated into all aspects of our lives (see chapter 8). Our faith calls us to serve. As we serve, we earn the rite for a hearing of the gospel in our community and beyond.

Dr. James Emery White said this about service – “In 1 Peter 4:10 the Bible says, ‘*God has given each of you a gift from his great variety of spiritual gifts. Use them well to serve one another.*’ The goal is to put yourself into play! And when we do that, we will reach a level of spiritual fulfillment, energy and passion that we can’t experience any other way. Holistic spiritual vitality and fulfillment can only come when we use our God-given, supernaturally empowered gifts in ministry.”[16] This sure sounds like thriving to me!

My friends leading Young Life in a wealthy San Francisco Bay area stumbled upon a valuable lesson. They found they could attract more unchurched teens to a week-long service project in Mexico than they could to a five-star Young Life camp. Afterall, their parents would take them to Hawaii or Cabo for family vacation, so the bells and whistles of a Young Life camp didn’t stir their hearts. But to venture to Tijuana to put new roofs on dilapidated houses appealed to their inner sensibility.

When the teens were asked how it felt to serve those poor families, they gushed, “It was fantastic!” This gave their leaders occasion to make the obvious connection that, “Since service felt so good, and Jesus instructed us to serve, do you think other things Jesus asks of us would also feel good? Let’s explore this together.” What a practical introduction to experiencing the gospel!

My dear brother in Christ, Kevin Bohli, has been the director of youth and young adult ministry for the Catholic diocese of Arlington, VA for over twenty years. Each summer, he and his leaders take 800 plus high school students to a weeklong Work Camp where they serve the poor within their own communities. He confirms that the touch with Jesus the youth experience through Work Camp is more profound than any other retreat he has seen. Kevin is convinced that service is a means to experience Jesus in a deeply personal way.

Jesus hit his listeners right between the eyes when he said, *Then the righteous will answer him, saying, 'Lord, when did we see you hungry and feed you, or thirsty and give you drink? And when did we see you a stranger and welcome you, or naked and clothe you? And when did we see you sick or in prison and visit you?' And the King will answer them, 'Truly, I say to you, as you did it to one of the least of these my brothers, you did it to me* (Matthew 25:37-40).

When we serve others, we are serving Jesus and actually experiencing His presence. We are His hands and feet.

Questions to Consider

1. When have you personally experienced the fulfillment that comes from serving someone? What motivated you to serve in this way?

2. Are you content with your level of service? If not, why do you not serve more regularly? What are some of your obstacles?

3. Do you believe this statement by James Emery White is true: "Holistic spiritual vitality and fulfillment can only come when we use our God-given, supernaturally empowered gifts in ministry." If so, how will you apply this to your life? Why not add these actions to "My Plan for Thriving."

CHAPTER 11

Be Proud of Your Story and Share it Freely

That which was from the beginning, which we have heard, which we have seen with our eyes, which we have looked at and our hands have touched—this we proclaim concerning the Word of life. The life appeared; we have seen it and testify to it, and we proclaim to you the eternal life, which was with the Father and has appeared to us.
1 John 1:1-2

Sing to the Lord...proclaim his salvation day after day. Declare his glory among the nations, his marvelous deeds among all peoples.
Psalm 96:2-3

We have met the King – go tell it on the mountain! Our heavenly Father made a way for us to come to know Him by sending Jesus to be the propitiation for our sins. The path that led us to Jesus is unique to each of us. That makes our story a wonderful thing to behold; a testament to God's faithfulness and relentless pursuit. Our upbringing, family dynamics, strengths and weaknesses, hardships and victories are all personal just to us. No wonder our path to finding Jesus is also uniquely personal.

There is certainly power in the gospel; His story. And, because of that, there is power in our stories as well. While most

Christians believe we are called to share our faith, (and that the fate of the Church depends on it!), less of us are actually fulfilling this calling on any sort of regular basis. In fact, most current research shows that 95% of believers will never lead a single person to Jesus in their lifetime. Yikes!!! There are many reasons for this, one being that our traditional tools for witnessing seem a bit outdated; even forced.

Unbelievers today don't want to be preached at or told they are going to Hell, but most are on a quest to discover a higher power. Our Jesus stories are not preaching. When we offer portions of our Jesus story into conversations with friends, we are simply sharing what is important to us and how God has revealed himself to us in a deeply personal way.

We don't need to unload our entire testimony each time we share. We can simply look for opportunities to insert a part of our story; one step at a time. Jim, a buddy of mine, recently remarked how sad it is that in conversations we tend to ask questions like, "How are you doing?" "What's new?" "How's the family?" which are all good questions because they show we care. But what about the more important questions we don't ask? If the key to thriving in life here and now, as well as in eternity, is whether or not we have surrendered to Jesus, doesn't it behoove us to ask one another some eternal questions? These sorts of questions open the door for parts of our testimony:

- Do you feel like you are living your best life? Do you have a clear sense of your purpose?
- What would you like your friends and family to say about you when they honor you in your senior years?
- As you navigate life these days, where do you see God? Is He involved with you at all?
- What do you think are the keys to a thriving life? Is faith an essential ingredient or not?

- What if what the Bible says is true? What are the consequences of that for how we are living?

- Do you think God is interested in being a part of our lives, or is He more concerned with other priorities?

- What do you believe it takes to make it to heaven when we die?

- How much of a priority is it for you to introduce your children to faith?

Our journey after meeting Jesus is as dynamic as our coming to Him. As a follower of Christ, the Holy Spirit imbues us with different gifts and specific missions for the various chapters of our lives. So, our testimonies are not merely a recounting of how we came to a personal relationship with Jesus. They should also reflect what we are learning currently and how Jesus is revealing Himself in fresh ways.

My co-father-in-law, Keith Rich, and I are building an elaborate treehouse for our grandchildren. Since it is attached to two different trees, it is important that hardware be inserted that allows the trees to continue to grow and sway in the wind as needed. Otherwise, the treehouse would eventually be torn apart. This special hardware is called "dynamic" because it allows for growth.

Like trees, if we cease to grow, we begin to slowly die. The Holy Spirit keeps us dynamic and changing as we grow into the image of our Lord. Let's pay attention to what the Spirit is doing in our lives and be intentional to share the joy of our journey with others.

As my friend "Pickle" shared with me, "the opportunities to touch others have always been there. It's just that I now see them thanks to God's Spirit illuminating me." Charles Hodge eloquently reminds us that "The design of redemption is to exhibit the grace of God in such a conspicuous manner as to fill all hearts with wonder and all lips with praise."[17]

Jesus assures us we are called to be His witnesses; every one of us. The key is to be prayerful each day to spot opportunities to insert bits of our story into conversations. My friend Manning begins each day with the following prayer: "Lord, allow me to be a blessing to at least one person today." The Lord assures us this is a prayer He wants to honor. *But you will receive power when the Holy Spirit comes on you; and you will be My witnesses in Jerusalem, and in all Judea and Samaria, and to the ends of the earth* (Acts 1:8).

While we may fear a presentation of the gospel could offend a lost or seeking friend, we can rest assured that our own stories likely will not. If social media has taught us anything, it is that people want to know and be known. We enjoy sharing and hearing stories with friends. Therefore, I encourage us to map out our testimony so we know it well enough to comfortably insert relevant pieces into conversations as they arise. (See "My Dynamic Story" worksheet in the appendix)

Our Witness is Both Verbal and Non-verbal

My friend, Bill Dalgetty, a founding member of Christians in Commerce, shared this from his experience as an attorney in a large multi-national company: "Our initial witness to Jesus Christ is usually better accomplished with conduct than with words. The conduct establishes the credibility and opens the door for the words to have more impact when the opportunity arises. The expression, 'talk is cheap' applies to Christians too. If you want the opportunity to witness to Christ with your words, witness first with your conduct."

In Young Life we call this non-verbal witnessing, "Earning the Right to be Heard." My first boss, Chuck Reinhold, used to say that we communicate 750 ways other than verbally (I never found a study substantiating this, but the point is good). Let your love show before your words flow. In 1 Corinthians 1:6 Paul teaches that our lives confirm our testimony about Jesus. Is that true for you? Does your life confirm or confuse that we are bearers of Jesus' name, and models of the dynamic new life He promises?

Bridges are constructed to attach two divided land masses. They are a means for someone on one side of a gulf to come over to the other. If we look for bridges in conversations that take us from a secular topic to something of a spiritual nature, we will find plenty of opportunities for imparting some of the wonders the Lord has done in our life. Our example of obedience, combined with our enthusiasm for Christ's inner working, are very compelling tools in our evangelistic arsenal.

Be a Proud and Grateful Witness

I found a recent post by Pastor James Emery White so moving that I wanted to summarize it here for us. I hope it moves you to action as it did me.

> Renown atheist, Penn Jillette, once said, "I don't respect people who don't proselytize…if you believe there is a heaven and hell and that people could be going to hell…how much would you have to hate them to not proselytize?"
>
> Dr. White asked the question:
>
> "What is the most important, strategic, life-changing

> thing you could ever do for another human being?" You could become a teacher and help the illiterate learn to read. You could become a doctor and heal the sick. You could enter politics and work to pass laws that protect the vulnerable and bring justice to the oppressed. You could join the military and defend our freedoms – all great causes and vitally important! But none are the greatest thing you could do for another person.
>
> The only investment we can make in another that blesses them, not only in this life, but for eternity, is to introduce them to their living Savior, Jesus Christ. This introduction brings new life, new purpose, new identity as a child of God, and a Kingdom perspective through which to view all of life. Not only is following Jesus our cherished calling, inviting others to follow Him is our commissioning.

Sadly, many of us (myself included) go years at a time without introducing a single person to faith in Christ. Half of millennial Christians think it is wrong to evangelize others. Do we not believe in eternal consequences, or is Penn Jillette right in saying we just don't care enough about other people to engage in risky conversations? I know neither is true of us. So, let's start praying for opportunities to share with those in our circle of influence, and look to join the Holy Spirit in this important work.

Turning Everyday Conversations Eternal

Nick Manos is a long-standing regional director in Young Life. He wrote the following from his many years of experience witnessing to lost teens:

In John 4, Jesus does something that is, as always, unbelievable. You know the story. Jesus travels through Samaria and goes in the middle of the day to get a drink of water from a well. While He is there, He meets a Samaritan woman who is also at the well to draw water. Jesus asks her for a drink. This begins a conversation about … water. But Jesus doesn't leave it there. He takes an everyday conversation about a drink of water and turns it eternal. Because Jesus doesn't just leave the conversation there, but instead takes it to a more substantial place, a woman's life is changed for eternity. And not just her life, but other lives in her hometown too. Simple, right? Well, not always.

This is a difficult maneuver for so many of us. But, what if we all took the everyday encounters with the people God puts in our paths and, like Jesus, turned everyday conversations eternal? What if we talked not only about important things, but the most important thing? Perhaps eternity hangs in the balance.

Tilling the Soil is Essential

Like dry, hard-packed soil, many people we know have hearts that are hardened to the gospel. Learning from the example of a patient farmer, believers need to skillfully till the soil to create a soft place for gospel seeds to land, take root, and grow. What might this spiritual tilling look like? Here are four time-tested methods modeled by our Lord and the Saints who have gone before us for cultivating hearts to receive the gospel:

1. **Prayer** – Jesus said, *If you remain in me and my words remain in you, ask whatever you wish, and it will be done for you. This is to my*

Father's glory, that you bear much fruit (John 15:7-8). One of the goals of intercessory prayer is for God to open the hearts of those with whom we hope to minister. There is no greater tool in our arsenal than prayer. *No one comprehends the thoughts of God except the Spirit of God...The natural person does not accept the things of the Spirit of God, for they are folly to him, and he is not able to understand them because they are spiritually discerned* (1 Corinthians 2:11, 14).

2. **Building relationships** – When we extend ourselves to greet a neighbor or the bank teller, or the checkout clerk at our weekly grocery store, we carry the fragrance of Jesus (2 Corinthians 2:14); and, over time, we earn the right to share the gospel. As they see the joy, peace, and purpose we hold dear they see something they desire. And, when they feel loved by us they get a taste of the love Jesus has for them. Hearts start to open. My pastor friend, Tom Pounder, teaches that good deeds can lead to God conversations, which can lead to gospel proclamation:

Good . God . Gospel.

3. **Love for One Another** – Jesus tells us the most compelling proof that the gospel is true is how we love one another in the body of Christ – *By this all people will know that you are My disciples, if you have love for one another* (John 13:35). Inviting seeking friends into our fellowship gives them a taste of the secret sauce that proves beyond a shadow of a doubt it is ALL TRUE!

4. **Sharing Your Story!**

Standing Strong in a Godless Culture

Tolerance is a cultural virtue that has received way too much affirmation over the past decade. Nowadays, folks prefer we keep religion and other potentially divisive opinions to themselves. "After all, what you believe is your truth and what I believe is my truth." Of course, this notion fails the logic test. Rather than leading as the Lord directs, believers today have succumbed to tolerance and abdicated their role as salt and light.

Michael Zigarelli, associate professor of management at the Charleston University School of Business, conducted a survey that confirmed a vicious cycle prompted by cultural conformity:[18]

1. Christians are assimilating a culture of busyness, hurry, and overload, which leads to…

2. God becoming more marginalized in Christians lives, which leads to…

3. A deteriorating relationship with God, which leads to…

4. Christians becoming even more vulnerable to adopting secular assumptions about how to live and what is right and wrong, which leads to…

5. More conformity to a culture of busyness, hurry, overload, and irrational thinking. And so it continues.

Jesus instructed His Church to be the salt of the earth and light of the world. Salt, in biblical times, served as both a spice and a preservative. The Church was entrusted to preserve God's ways and his teachings in society. Our Constitution and Bill of Rights were inspired by biblical teachings, as were most of the laws in our land. They serve as a light to all – beacons of truth, appealing to our inner sensibilities, and offering us peace. Sadly, the masses now view God as antiquated, out of touch with reality. Even worse, many view God, or at least Christians, as hate-filled, bigoted, or homophobic, so they throw the baby out with the bathwater.

Forty million Americans have stopped attending church in the past 25 years. That's about 12 percent of the population, and it represents the largest concentrated change in church attendance in American history.[19] No wonder chaos is on the rise and morality is being shelved. *The fool says in his heart, "There is no God." They are corrupt, they do abominable deeds; there is none who does good* (Psalm 14:1). Those in our circles of influence need to know that Jesus has a better way and our testimonies to that fact are vital.

What is the Remedy?

When the crowd in the Apostle Peter's time asked what they should do in response to the corruption in their generation, Peter replied, *Repent and be baptized, every one of you, in the name of Jesus Christ for the forgiveness of your sins; and you will receive the gift of the Holy Spirit. He went on to say that this promise is for you and your children and for all who are far off—for all the Lord our God will call* (Acts 2:38-39). That includes you and me!

Though Peter's words were directed at the people in front of him, they are in fact timeless, applicable to generations beyond his own. The loss of respect for life in our current day, the confusion over truth, the erosion of integrity, the diminishing state of sexual morality, all point to corruption in our present generation. A call to personal as well as corporate repentance is the need of our day. Let it begin with me!

I'll close this chapter with pastor Rick Warren's commitment to standing firm on the rock of his foundation – "A Call to Radical Commitment" by Rick Warren.

> "Today I am stepping across the line. I'm tired of waffling, and I'm finished with wavering. I've made my choice; the verdict is in; and my decision is irrevocable. I'm going God's way. There's no turning back now!
>
> I will live the rest of my life serving God's purposes with God's people on God's planet for God's glory. I will use my life to celebrate his presence, cultivate his character, participate in his family, demonstrate his love, and communicate his Word.
>
> Since my past has been forgiven, and I have a purpose for living and a home awaiting in heaven, I refuse to waste any more time or energy on shallow living, petty thinking, trivial talking, thoughtless doing, useless regretting, hurtful resenting, or faithless worrying.
>
> Instead I will magnify God, grow to maturity, serve in ministry, and fulfill my mission in the membership of his family.
>
> Because this life is preparation for the next, I will value worship over wealth, "we" over "me," character over comfort, service over status, and people over possessions, position, and pleasures. I know what matters most, and I'll give it all I've got. I'll do the best I can with what I have for Jesus Christ today.

I won't be captivated by culture, manipulated by critics, motivated by praise, frustrated by problems, debilitated by temptation, or intimidated by the devil. I'll keep running my race with my eyes on the goal, not the sidelines or those running by me.

When times get tough, and I get tired, I won't back up, back off, back down, back out, or backslide. I'll just keep moving forward by God's grace. I'm Spirit-led, purpose-driven and mission-focused, so I cannot be bought, I will not be compromised, and I shall not quit until I finish the race.

I'm a trophy of God's amazing grace, so I will be gracious to everyone, grateful for everyday, and generous with everything that God entrusts to me.

To my Lord and Savior Jesus Christ, I say: However, whenever, wherever, and whatever you ask me to do, my answer in advance is yes! Wherever you lead and whatever the cost, I'm ready. Anytime. Anywhere. Anyway.

Whatever it takes Lord; whatever it takes!

I want to be used by you in such a way, that on that final day I'll hear you say, "Well done, thou good and faithful one. Come on in, and let the eternal party begin!" [20]

Processing This Chapter

1. Take 15 minutes to begin outlining the story of your journey to and with Jesus by answering the questions in My Dynamic Story in the appendix.

2. What holds you back from sharing your story with friends, family or neighbors? How can you remedy this?

3. What Good News have you experienced you would be excited to pass on to others?

4. In My Plan for Thriving, make a Prospect List of people with whom you, in faith, plan to share your story. Begin praying for them and watch how opportunities avail themselves.

CHAPTER 12

Be a Multiplier

Therefore go and make disciples of all nations, baptizing them in the name of the Father and of the Son and of the Holy Spirit, and teaching them to obey everything I have commanded you. And surely I am with you always, to the very end of the age.

Matthew 28:19-20

And the things you have heard me say in the presence of many witnesses entrust to reliable people who will also be qualified to teach others.
2 Timothy 2:2

A Tree is Known by its Fruit

I remember so vividly when our youngest daughter was just hours from delivering our first grandbaby – a little boy Kris and I were ecstatic to meet! It is so exciting seeing our offspring now reproducing children of their own. We currently have six grandchildren and keep our fingers crossed more may still be in the works! I picture our Creator grinning with gleeful anticipation as we follow His command to, *Be fruitful and multiply* (Genesis 1:28)!

Production, more than reproduction, is a huge theme in American culture. We are proud to be producers and exporters of goods and services. We measure the value of individuals by their production; the contributions they make toward the bottom line. Employers are constantly on the lookout for producers, people who will be "difference-makers." And, as these competent men and women move up the ladder, they become reproducers of other leaders in the organization.

In ministry, we are motivated by production as well. In this case, our focus is the production of disciples of Jesus. We labor diligently to equip young believers to feed themselves spiritually so they can stand firm in their faith. Introducing people to Jesus, as incredible as that is, does not alone fulfill the Great Commission. We are tasked to make disciples – Christ followers who are able to stand the test of time and reproduce their faith in others. Evangelism and discipleship are two equal and vital parts of salvation – a process requiring a variety of investments as led by the Holy Spirit.

In many churches, our 21st Century picture of a disciple has drifted from what Jesus modeled with his original twelve. The saying goes, "You know a tree by its fruit." What was the fruit of Jesus' discipleship? It was a team of eleven who reproduced not only other followers of Jesus, but other producers of followers of Jesus. They developed women and men with the vision, gifts, and skills to not only produce converts, but reproduce leaders, pastors, elders, and priests. This is the fruit Jesus envisioned we would offer Him –*...some thirty, some sixty, some a hundred times what was sown* (Mark 4:20). The movement they built has impacted billions in nearly every corner of the world and continues to do so today.

Are You Ready to Reproduce?

What might be holding you back? Answer this statement true or false: "We will only take others as far as we have gone ourselves in Christ." We need to not only know, but be living the gospel before we can effectively reproduce it in others. Much more will be caught than taught by our mentees. Let's be sure to be investing in our own journey with the Lord on a daily basis so we have fresh fuel to be giving away to others. As I mentioned before, there is nothing in this world more important than our own personal walk with Jesus; nothing.

Gleaning from the Parable of the Sower

Discipleship is not a meeting or curriculum; it requires a long-term investment in people. Listen to Jesus' explanation of the parable of the sower: *When anyone hears the message about the kingdom and does not understand it, the evil one comes and snatches away what was sown in their heart. This is the seed sown along the path. The seed falling on rocky ground refers to someone who hears the word and at once receives it with joy. But since they have no root, they last only a short time. When trouble or persecution comes because of the word, they quickly fall away. The seed falling among the thorns refers to someone who hears the word, but the worries of this life and the deceitfulness of wealth choke the word, making it unfruitful. But the seed falling on good soil refers to someone who hears the word and understands it. This is the one who produces a crop, yielding a hundred, sixty or thirty times what was sown* (Matthew 13:18-23).

The first seed that fails to plant is the result of insufficient tilling of the soil. We have already addressed strategies to eradicate this. The second seed receives the gospel quickly but doesn't develop deep roots sufficient to sustain it through trials and persecution. It is so important that our newly excited believers get planted in fellowship quickly and connect with peers who will encourage their walk with Christ. Small groups are terrific for this! The second seed also reminds us of the importance of teaching young believers how to meet the Lord in the Scriptures and connect with Him in prayer. They must be skilled at feeding their faith (see chapters 4 and 5).

The third seed confirms the need for spiritual leaders to take a long view of discipleship. Weeds don't spring up immediately but over time, and they manifest themselves uniquely in each person. We may need to help our disciples prune some things in their lives that are holding back their growth in Christ. Some of these things are obviously harmful – bad habits, unhealthy relationships, and immoral behavior. Some might be good things that are wrongly prioritized like perhaps work or money, or the love of a sport. There is nothing wrong with liking to play golf; unless it becomes such a compulsion that family time is squandered, or an irresponsible amount of money is spent on it. The term all things in moderation reverberates here. Nothing should take center stage in our lives other than Jesus. Anything else will choke us and hold back the multiplication of fruit.

Along the way it is helpful to apply some fertilizer in the form of affirmation and encouragement. You won't have much competition for being someone who encourages the positive steps you see your disciples take toward Jesus. They need to be reminded they are honoring the Lord's intent for them and will be blessed as a result. Affirmation will help your sprouts endure the cold of winter and become the fourth seed that reproduces a crop of their own.

Setting the Bar Too Low

I have felt challenged lately that my prayers and practice have too often settled at helping disciples grow in their faith, or perhaps actively witness to others, but has stopped short of investing in them with a vision to become leaders of leaders. Should we not be looking for men and women with the gifts and character to be reproducers of other Kingdom leaders? Might the next Mother Theresa or Billy Graham be right in front of us? What a shame if we lower the bar and cease to disciple them once they have checked a few introductory boxes like, plugging into a church and having regular quiet times.

Mark Twain is credited with the story of a man who died and met Saint Peter at the gates of heaven. Knowing that Peter was very wise, he asked a question that he had wondered about his whole life. He said: "I have been interested in military history for many years. Read everything I could, studied it, went to battlefields and walked the grounds. Who was the greatest general of all time?"

Peter replied: "Oh, that's easy. It's that man right over there." The man looked over and he knew him! He said: "You have to be mistaken. I knew that man on Earth. He was just a common, everyday man—he managed a store near my house." To which Peter said: "That's right. But he would have been the greatest general of all time, if he had been a general."

By God's grace, some of you have already become Kingdom Reproducers. A great opportunity awaits us all as we raise the bar to envision, pray, and invest in a few leaders with tremendous potential to be Kingdom reproducers themselves. *Go and bear fruit—fruit that will last* (John 15:16).

To Summarize

What is indispensable to fruitfulness? Sow the right seed, prepare the soil well, tend to our young plants, fertilize often, prune when needed, and give them vision to reproduce a crop – thirty, sixty, or a hundredfold. Clearly, <u>discipleship is not a short course, but a long-term commitment</u>.

Questions for Processing:

1. What fruit have you produced so far with God's help? Is your standard for fruitfulness in keeping with the Lord's, or have you set your bar too low?

2. What steps will you implement this year to potentially increase your harvest and bless those you lead?

3. How confident do you feel to be producing, not just converts, but disciples who are leaders of leaders? Where do you need to grow?

4. In My Plan for Thriving, list a couple of people you might initiate mentoring or discipling this year. When will you reach out to them with an invitation?

CHAPTER 13

Engage in Authentic Community

How good and pleasant it is when God's people live together in unity!
Psalm 133:1

And let us consider how we may spur one another on toward love and good deeds, not giving up meeting together, as some are in the habit of doing, but encouraging one another—and all the more as you see the Day approaching.
Hebrews 10:24-25

Let's face it, we were not built to navigate through life alone. Regardless of whether you land on the introvert scale, or if you are an extreme extravert, we all need and want community – and not just superficial friends. We want to do life with people who know us well and love us anyhow! We were built for community: for family, friends, and yes, we were built for the Church!

The hours invested today on social media confirm we all want to know and be known. We yearn for friends we can count on to love us even when our faults are blatantly evident. We want "likes" and "ata boys" as they blow wind in our sails. Our social media experience also confirms that our level of interaction with friends online is an epic failure in terms of providing authentic community. How might you describe "authentic" community? What does it look like, and where can it be found?

Authentic means real, not an imitation. That's easy to agree on. But what does real community consist of? I suggest it is a group of people defined by their commitment to one another, and their pursuit of a similar set of desired ends. This can be neighbors raising kids together, or colleagues on a work team. Fraternities and sororities depict these ingredients. We work together because we need each other. This commonality allows us to overlook minor shortcomings for the sake of the greater good.

Sports teams, dance troops, and other focused group activities give us experiences, both hard and good, with real community. They teach us to stack hands together to achieve our desired result. Working hard to accomplish agreed upon objectives teaches teammates to respect and encourage their fellow players. The sum of the whole is dependent on the well-being of each of its parts.

Rabbi David Schiff defines authentic community this way: "Authentic community is a space where we feel safe to discuss significant issues honestly, knowing we will be seen and loved; where we don't need to agree, and don't even want to agree; where we respect each other enough to appreciate each other for our differences."[21]

The hit sitcom Friends was wildly popular for a similar reason. Here were six very different people who, rather than critiquing one another, chose to accept each other's quirks without judgement or any bearing on their friendship. Millions of viewers yearned for a fellowship like theirs.

Unconditional acceptance is but one aspect of authentic community. When a common mission is added to the mix, like winning a championship, or rebuilding the neighbor's house that was flooded, or reaching your school for Christ, the sense of community is further heightened. When the steaks transcend this world into eternity, there is nothing that can compare to the mutual commitment shared by believers striving together. Do you see the need for the Church?

Grace-filled Relationships = True Community

The Apostle James underscores what a blessing it is to commit to the spiritual well-being of a brother or sister: *My brothers and sisters, if one of you should wander from the truth and someone should bring that person back, remember this: Whoever turns a sinner from the error of their way will save them from death and cover over a multitude of sins* (James 5:19-20). We all need someone like this to whom we are accountable.

In Young Life we have Campaigners groups, which at their core are small group Bible studies. The teens involved have a high level of commitment to attendance because Campaigners is a place where they feel safe to share their questions, and even their weaknesses, with peers who support them regardless. They seek to spur on their friends in their mutual pursuit of Jesus. This group is also united by their desire to build a dynamic Young Life club at their school and invite their friends to participate – another example where a common mission fosters community.

I submit that the truest expression of authentic community is found among people who strive to live as Jesus taught; His church. Listen to this description of the earliest church in action: *They devoted themselves to the apostles' teaching and to fellowship, to the breaking of bread and to prayer. Everyone was filled with awe at the many wonders and signs performed by the apostles. All the believers were together and had every-*

thing in common. They sold property and possessions to give to anyone who had need. Every day they continued to meet together in the temple courts. They broke bread in their homes and ate together with glad and sincere hearts, praising God and enjoying the favor of all the people. And the Lord added to their number daily those who were being saved (Acts 2:42-47).

Please don't confuse this text as a treatise for socialism – it is not! I share it in light of this discussion because it shows practical ways God's people were relating to one another in their respective communities. They shared meals, worked together, worshipped, and served. I'm sure their kids played together, and they committed to the mutual thriving of their neighbors and community at large. Who wouldn't want to be part of a community like this?

Jesus had various circles of intimacy with His disciples: the most inner circle were the three (Peter, James and John), then there were the twelve, then in the next ring outward there were the 72 disciples in close enough proximity to represent Jesus on a missionary journey (see Luke 10). There were also the five hundred brothers and sisters to whom Jesus appeared following His resurrection.

As we think about the authentic community we desire, I suspect we envision similar circles of connection. We only have time and emotional energy to be "best friends" with so many people. These relationships demand regular, consistent investment. But then there is the next circle of people we enjoy that we invest in frequently, but less often than our inner circle. And so it goes.

The Gift of Covenant Friendship

How good and pleasant it is when God's people live together in unity! It is like precious oil poured on the head, running down on the beard, running down on Aaron's beard, down on the collar of his robe. It is as if the dew of Hermon were falling on Mount Zion. For there the Lord bestows his blessing, even life forevermore (Psalm 133:1-3).

Jonathan and David are one of the most famous pictures of friends becoming spiritual brothers. Their relationship went to a level unfamiliar to mortal man apart from the movement of God. Samuel describes their relationship this way: *Jonathan and David became bound together in close friendship, and Jonathan began to love him as himself. And Jonathan made a covenant with David because he loved him as himself. What is more, Jonathan and David made a covenant, a solemn agreement that bound them together as friends who would support each other* (I Samuel 18:1-5). Furthermore, Jonathan said to David, *'Go in peace, because we have sworn both of us in the name of the Lord, saying, 'The Lord shall be between me and you, and between my offspring and your offspring, forever* (1 Sa 20:42).'

When Jesus comes into the center of already strong friendships, it takes the parties from being mere buddies, to brothers or sisters in Christ. Not only does this transformation from within lead to more in-depth fellowship, it actually causes one to commit to the spiritual success of the other. For example, when your friend goes off to college, you hound them until they engage in Christian fellowship there. Or, if they decide to go to a party where they might be tempted, you go with them. In this way, you fulfill the exhortation of Hebrews 10:24-25 at the top of this chapter.

On their last night before the crucifixion, Jesus reinforced this theme to His disciples: *Greater love has no one than this: to lay down one's life for one's friends* (John 15:13). Do you have a friend or group of friends with whom you share this sort of commitment? If not, wouldn't you like to? I believe everyone wants and needs some brothers or sisters with whom they can be completely genuine, open and honest, supportive of, and share the ups and downs of life. Since we all seek this, it behooves each of us to take initiative and reach out to a friend with this idea. There is no right or wrong way to forge a covenant friendship – we are each free to follow the path that feels right to us.

A popular saying attributed to Aesop is, "We are known by the company we keep." Listen to what Solomon, the wisest man who ever lived had to say about this – *Join the company of good men and women, keep your feet on the tried-and-true paths. It's the men who walk straight who will settle this land, the women with integrity who will last here* (Proverbs 2:20).

A faithful friend is a sure shelter, whoever finds one has found a rare treasure. A faithful friend is something beyond price, there is no measuring his worth. A faithful friend is the elixir of life, and those who fear the Lord will find one. Whoever fears the Lord makes true friends, for as a man is, so is his friend (Ecclesiasticus 6:14-17, included in the Apocrypha).

I am blessed to have several covenant friends that I would do anything for. One is John Colston, my best friend since the 7th grade. As young teens we enjoyed horsing around and playing sports. But later in high school we both were introduced to a personal relationship with Jesus through our involvement in Young Life. This commitment took our friendship from being mere buddies to brothers in Christ. John helps me in the pursuit of my goals, he encourages me in my ministry pursuits, he asks how my marriage is going and what he can pray for. And I do the same for him. It is comforting to know there is someone committed to my thriving and loves me enough to ask the hard questions. I am free (and encouraged) not only to share my joys with John, but my struggles and sins as well. With John I am free to be myself. This accountability helps spur me on in my spiritual growth.

I suspect most of us reading this have a friend that comes to mind who could become a covenant friend if not so already. It only takes one person to initiate to go to the next level. Will you take this step?

Questions to Consider

1. When have you experienced Authentic community as described in this chapter? If so, what was unique about it?

2. Have you had the opportunity to minister with a community of friends? How did their fellowship empower your witness?

3. How do you understand a Covenant Relationship? Do you already have such a relationship, or do you have someone in mind you might approach to begin? Note any actions for follow through in My Plan for Thriving.

CHAPTER 14

Our Call to the Church (Why is it needed?)

So that we may present everyone
fully mature in Christ.
Colossians 1:28

But in fact God has placed the parts in the body, every one of them, just as he wanted them to be. If they were all one part, where would the body be? As it is, there are many parts, but one body. Now you are the body of Christ and individually members of it.
1 Corinthians 12:19-20, 27

Any study you read today sends a troubling picture of declining church attendance in America, especially among younger generations. Regardless of its challenges, the Church holds the keys to spiritual flourishing in society, and is vital for the thriving of individual believers.

Jesus established the church as a necessary institution for the good of His people. Paul uses the metaphor of the body in 1 Corinthians 12 to emphasize that individual Christians need to be connected to other individual Christians. Head, shoulders, knees, and toes—they all depend upon each other. The Holy Spirit gives different gifts that when brought together, bring the power to redeem a lost world.

Doing life together with fellow believers strengthens our resolve to stand strong in the midst of a godless culture. Jesus tells us in John 15 that He is like a vine and we are like branches on that vine. If we disconnect we die. We need the Lord, and we need each other. We flourish when committed to one another, and the world around us is blessed by the witness of our community. In fact, Jesus said that the key ingredient to our witness is how believers love one another. Here is my interpretation of this conversation Jesus had with his disciples following the Last Supper: [bracketed phrases are my interpretation of what the disciples were thinking]

Jesus said, *A new command I give you:* [the disciples all lean in to listen] *Love one another* [what's new about this? We were told by Moses hundreds of years ago to love each other]. *As I have loved you, so you must love one another* [Oh, that answers my first question. Your love for us is other-worldly. Yet, your consistent example has been so tangible that we at least have a picture now to shoot for. And, we know you are going to give us the Holy Spirit to help us succeed]. *By this everyone will know that you are my disciples, if you love one another* (John 13:34-35). [Wait, did you really say 'everyone?' That's a lot of people. We're talking entire world impact if we love each other the way you loved us – unconditionally, patiently, consistently, sacrificially, then the entire world will be reached? This even transcends time - Wow! I'm ALL-IN for that, what about you guys]?

The Covid pandemic forced most believers to stay home on Sundays versus risking their health to be in Church. Sadly, many who grew accustomed to lounging at home on Sundays never went back to church after Covid passed. We can convince ourselves of loads of reasons to make church involvement optional, but they are merely frivolous justifications – "I don't get much out of the sermon," "The worship isn't my style," "I don't see a space where I want to serve," "My doctrinal stances have changed so I want to find a church that resonates with my evolved thinking." You can fill in the blank for what you have heard or perhaps felt yourself.

John Mark Comer offers the illustration of a trellis to further depict Jesus' metaphor of the vine and branches. "For a vine to 'bear much fruit,' what does it need? A Trellis – a support structure to lift it off the ground and index it toward the light, give it room to breathe, and guide its growth in the desired direction. Without a trellis's support, the vine would bear a fraction of the fruit it's capable of, and the little it did bear would be highly vulnerable to disease, damage, and dangerous predators."[22] The Church is our trellis.

Why do we Need the Church?

1. It is in the Church where we discover our gifts. Lebron James didn't know he had basketball talent until he played with others.

2. We need authority. That is the way God designed us. We are not all free to interpret Scripture any way we like. Our early church fathers gave their lives for the sake of producing the canon of Scripture. Pastors attend seminary to learn how to responsibly interpret and teach the Scriptures to those less learned. Doctrine matters.

3. We never cease to be in need of grace. Sinners need a place to repent, be restored, and heal from the spiritual battle. The sacraments of the Church meet these needs. Baptism is an important outward expression of our surrender to Jesus.

4. We need more than just our peers. Author Christian Smith's research found that, "One of the clearest indicators of whether a teen will remain in the faith as a young adult is how many adults in the church they know by name."[23] Our personal thriving is inextricably linked to the thriving of Christ's body. Let's invest well in the Church to see it be all that it can be!

Questions to Consider

1. Discuss some of the strengths and weaknesses of the Church today from your vantage point? What step(s) could you take to help the church flourish? Consider adding a goal related to this to My Plan for Thriving.

2. What gifts do you bring to the body of Christ? How are you investing those gifts currently?

3. If you were running a church what would you do differently?

Chapter 15

Strive to Excel
No Benchwarmers!

Be very careful, then, how you live—not as unwise but as wise, making the most of every opportunity, because the days are evil.
Ephesians 5:15-16

Therefore, my dear brothers and sisters, stand firm. Let nothing move you. Always give yourselves fully to the work of the Lord because you know that your labor in the Lord is not in vain.
1 Corinthians 15:58

I knew from the first time I held a paint brush in kindergarten that art was not going to be my thing. Finger dexterity and special relationships were not my forte. I liked art others did, but I would never excel there. I picked up a basketball and knew it was a much better fit.

Clearly, the Lord has gifted us each differently and intends for us to excel in our unique niches. Nobody wants a participation ribbon when a trophy can be earned! Future Hall of Fame NASCAR driver, Kyle Busch, was once asked by an interviewer how he felt about coming in second place after a long and grueling race. Busch replied, "Second place is like kissing your sister." Enough said!

I resonate with what Paul said in the verse above to give of myself fully to the work of the Lord. I played soccer in college, and know what it is like to "leave it all on the field." You go home tired yet gratified, and you look forward to the next game where you'll give your all again. This principle applies to most aspects of our lives. If you're a student, apply yourself diligently. If you're a husband or wife, keep investing in your marriage so you continually improve. If you're working, show your employer you are growing in your competency and eager to apply yourself to the tasks at hand. Just as plants begin to die if they cease to grow, so, too, do we begin to die if we cease to grow.

The research of Apollo Technical revealed that only 65% of US employees are satisfied with their jobs, and only 20% are passionate about their work.[24] While no job is enjoyable all the time, believers can change how they feel about their work by viewing work through a Kingdom lens. Why should church pastors be the only ones "called" to their jobs? How much of ourselves do we give to our work? A ton!!! Every job contributes to the economy and community, so every job is important. We need lawyers, garbage collectors, judges, waiters and waitresses, dry cleaners, teachers, bankers and small business owners to all do their best to make our communities prosper.

Most companies perform employee evaluations at least annually. This is where supervisors point out the contributions an employee has made to the overall health of the enterprise. Their growth and competency is affirmed, and areas needing improvement are discussed so they can develop a performance improvement plan. It feels good to be affirmed for our contributions. These pats on the back come most often when we heed Paul's advice – *Whatever you do, work heartily, as for the Lord and not for men* (Col 3:23).

The Great Commission gave Jesus' disciples vision for a task far beyond their own abilities. It would require their full devotion and then some. Even though the Holy Spirit is the one who will produce the fruit, Jesus' disciples are invited to participate wholeheartedly in His work of redeeming a lost world. We are the hands and feet of the Holy Spirit.

We are the hands and feet of the Holy Spirit.

Hall of Fame NFL coach, Vince Lombardi, believed each player must make a personal commitment to excellence. He coached that perfection was the goal, but, knowing perfection is impossible, a commitment to it would at least lead to excellence. His record gives credibility to those words. In his nine seasons with the Green Bay Packers, Lombardi's team won five NFL championships. Remarkable! I wonder what standard of excellence we use to measure and motivate our pursuit of Kingdom business?

Dave Alpern is the president of the Joe Gibbs Racing NASCAR team. In his book, "Taking the Lead: Winning Business Principles That Fuel Joe Gibbs Racing," Dave shares advice for how to make a difference in one's work. He says, "Be a fountain, not a drain. We hold 100-percent control over whether we will be a fountain (someone who breathes life and energy into a situation) or a drain (someone who drains resources adding only few)."[25] We want to create more value than either our pay or job description expects. Since these accomplishments are connected to Jesus being in the center of every part of our lives, they become part of our testimony.

Whether it be scholastic pursuits, work, friendships, marriages, hobbies, sports, you name it, we want to experience the just fruits of our labor. We want to be proud of our accomplishments. The good news is the Lord wants to see us thrive as well! *He came to prosper us, not to harm us, and to give us a hope and a future* (Jeremiah 29:11). The key is inviting Him into all of the many facets of our lives (see chapter 8).

When we examine our priorities, there really should be nothing on our plate more important than fulfilling our Heavenly calling to be a disciple of Jesus who reflects the Lord's character wherever we go. Jesus told his prospective followers, *Whoever wants to be my disciple must deny themselves and take up their cross daily and follow me* (Luke 9:23). Either we are All IN or we are not IN AT ALL! There are no benchwarmers in the Kingdom of God!

Excelling in What Matters Most
Developing Christ-like Character

In Paul's first letter to the Thessalonians he makes a point to affirm this young church for being leaders throughout Macedonia in living out their Christian character. He also points out how wonderfully they are loving each other. Rather than letting them sit back and be comfortable with these accomplishments, Paul exhorts them to "Excel still more!" Listen to this:

Finally then, brothers and sisters, we request and urge you in the Lord Jesus, that as you received instruction from us as to how you ought to walk and please God (just as you actually do walk), that you excel even more. Now as to the love of the brothers and sisters, you have no need for anyone to write to you, for you yourselves are taught by God to love one another; for indeed you practice it toward all the brothers and sisters who are in all Macedonia. But we urge you, brothers and sisters, to excel even more... (1 Thes 4:1, 9-10).

Christ-like character is formed by "practicing together," a phrase that came out of Fuller Youth Institute's research.[26] Head knowledge, if not applied with our feet and hands, soon becomes lost knowledge. It is as we experiment and try-on Christ's attitudes and actions that we grow more into His image. It is so important that whenever we read Scripture we ask: "So what?" How can I apply this lesson to my life this week?

Head knowledge, if not applied with our feet and hands, soon becomes lost knowledge.

I remember a particular Young Life Campaigners meeting when I was in high school where we studied Jesus' example of being a servant leader. Our leader challenged each of us to write down the name of someone we would serve that week. When we gather the following week we will share how our experiences went. I chose my mother to serve but had no idea what I would do.

My mother was a stay at home mom and served our family by making dinner and cleaning up afterwards, so I'm embarrassed to say I had never done the dinner dishes. One night this particular week my parents had to run out to a meeting immediately after dinner before mom had time to do the dishes. I saw my chance – so I looked up some instructions for how to wash dishes. When my mother returned, she about had a heart attack because the dishes had been cleaned and put away.

Who did this application from Bible study benefit? Certainly my mother. She saw a change of heart in me as a result of my newly developed relationship with Jesus. But more than even her, I was changed. I saw myself as the hands and feet of Jesus and it really felt good. Application spurred me on to want to continually put into practice the things Jesus taught.

Making Faith Stick

In youth ministry we see too many kids "fall with a great crash" as the years pass. We lose many when they graduate and move on to college or into the working world. Our Catholic friends see the majority of young people stop attending church following their confirmation. What can be done to reverse this trend and help make faith stick?

Timothy Witmer, in his book, The Shepherd Leader, speaks to the role of elders in the church as shepherds of the flock. He says, "A sheep retained is as valuable as a sheep gained, and well-shepherded sheep do not stray."[27] Elders are charged to keep sheep from straying and to notice when they do so they can urge them back into the fold.

The key ingredient has to be RELATIONSHIPS. We were not built to navigate life or faith alone. We need people to walk with, to encourage us, to correct and hold us accountable. Employees are motivated by performance improvement plans because they help them grow. We in the Church should exhort our brothers and sisters in similar fashion, but motivated by love, not production.

These sorts of friends should be in the inner circles of our personal communities. It is natural to have an older friend to mentor us during our early years following Jesus. What is critically important is for those leaders to stay connected to their mentees when they move on to the next phase of life. It is such a privilege to have witnessed the college graduations, weddings, and births of children of my former Young Life kids. Lee Corder, one of my first mentors, began investing vision in me as a senior in college. He is still doing that now over forty years later! Relational connection blesses people on both ends!

Questions to Consider

1. Is there a younger believer you have invested in that could use a call or cup of coffee now?

2. How conscientious are you to be looking for practical application from your Bible study? What difference could it make?

3. How confident do you feel about your ability to feed yourself spiritually? How can you grow in this area? (Note this in My Plan for Thriving)

4. Do you have a community of friends who spur you on in Christ? If not, who might you tap for this mutually beneficial role?

Chapter 16

Put up a Wall to Defeat the Enemy

Be alert and of sober mind. Your enemy the devil prowls around like a roaring lion looking for someone to devour.
1 Peter 5:8

Blessed is the one who perseveres under trial because, having stood the test, that person will receive the crown of life that the Lord has promised to those who love him.
James 1:12

Finally, be strong in the Lord and in his mighty power. Put on the full armor of God, so that you can take your stand against the devil's schemes. For our struggle is not against flesh and blood, but against the rulers, against the authorities, against the powers of this dark world and against the spiritual forces of evil in the heavenly realms.
Ephesians 6:10-12

In earlier centuries, cities small and large were fortified by high walls intended to protect the "good" people inside, and keep "bad" people from attacking. One of the most famous walls in the Old Testament is portrayed in the book of Nehemiah. The prophet Nehemiah was tasked by God to rebuild the wall that had been broken down in Jerusalem which made God's people vulnerable to attack. These walls symbolize a spiritual barrier to protect believers from the cultural norms of unbelievers that stand in opposition to God's design. God knew our moral discernment alone would not be up to the task.

Listen to what happens when God's people get it wrong by trying to fit into secular society:

> Ezra 9:1-2 – *...The people of Israel and the priests and the Levites have not separated themselves from the peoples of the lands with their abominations... For they have taken some of their daughters to be wives for themselves and for their sons, so that the holy race has mixed itself with the peoples of the lands.*

> Exodus 34:12-16 – *Take care, lest you make a covenant with the inhabitants of the land to which you go, lest it become a snare in your midst. You shall tear down their altars and break their pillars and cut down their Asherim (for you shall worship no other god, for the Lord, whose name is Jealous, is a jealous God), lest you make a covenant with the inhabitants of the land...*

A more thorough overview of Scripture makes it clear that God does not want His people living in little protective enclaves separated from society. We are called to be lights in the midst of darkness; to live in the world but not be of the world; and to make disciples of all nations. We are Christ's ambassadors living in a foreign land. We are not to lower our guard for the sake of blending in, or even for the more noble purpose of earning the right to be heard for a hearing of the gospel with neighbors.

Pure evil is being allowed to run unchecked, and the church has lost much of its cultural authority to suppress it. Christians are blending in more to culture rather than standing out and pointing the way. John the Apostle left us an important reminder on which to hang our hats: *You, dear children, are from God and have overcome them, because the one who is in you is greater than the one who is in the world* (1 John 4:4).

Where have you experienced spiritual attack? Is it in the form of persecution, temptation, relational tension, jealousy of others? All of these are standard fare for our enemy, so we must be ready for them.

How do we arm ourselves for the looming spiritual battles? We talked about the value of a Covenant Friend in chapter 13. The Apostle Paul explains some additional armor at our disposal for overcoming the devil's schemes. Let's briefly breakdown the seven pieces of armor Paul mentions in Ephesians chapter six:

> 1) Stand firm then, with the belt of truth buckled around your waist – One of the marks of postmodernism is people defining truth for themselves. They base their conclusions on their feelings and what they would like to be true. Today's younger churchgoers have been called, "Doctrinally Illiterate" by some. They love Jesus but have not been exposed to the creeds, prayers, and ancient hymns that repetitively impart the core doctrines of the faith. When these are absent the young believer lacks a foundation upon which to stand when confronted by false teaching. As a result, many deconstruct their faith and lean into what their secular friends are saying. It is critical that we know what we believe so we can defend it.

2) With the breastplate of righteousness in place – The breastplate was a metal encasing that protected the organs most needed to survive – the heart, lungs, liver, and kidneys. The heart is a big theme in the scriptures as it is mentioned more than 800 times. Jesus taught that, *A good person brings good things out of the good stored up in their heart, and an evil person brings evil things out of the evil stored up in their heart. For out of the overflow of the heart the mouth speaks* (Luke 6:45). And, Solomon in his wisdom admonishes us to, *Above all else guard your heart, for it is the wellspring of life* (Poverbsr 4:23).

How do you think we might practically guard our heart? For me, it is disciplining my inputs – what I take in with my eyes and listen to with my ears. If I am seeing and hearing messages that are contrary to my beliefs, and enjoying them for entertainment, then my heart for Christ is being doused with cold water rather than fueled. I also like to speak truths that remind me of the indescribable privilege I have to be counted a follower of Christ. So, words of affirmation, praying the creeds and Lord's prayer, and conversing with fellow believers helps sure up potential leaks.

3) With your feet fitted with the readiness that comes from the gospel of peace – *How beautiful are the feet of those who bring good news* (Romans 10:15b). We are called to lace up our shoes and boldly take the gospel of peace to those still searching (1 Peter 3:15). Witnessing draws us to plant our feet in the truth more firmly as we rely on God's Spirit for strength, clarity, and an open heart in our listeners. Don't fall

into the trap of winning the right to be heard and then re-winning the right... It's time to be heard!

4) Take up the shield of faith, with which you can extinguish all the flaming arrows of the evil one – Our faith can guard us during trials in the same way a shield does in battle. For example, when doubt creeps in or our beliefs are challenged, our faith in Christ draws us back to what we know to be true. In this way, our faith protects us as a shield; we deflect the attacks of our enemy. *Yet he did not waver through unbelief regarding the promise of God, but was strengthened in his faith and gave glory to God, being fully persuaded that God had power to do what he had promised* (Romans 4:20-21).

5) Take the helmet of salvation – The assurance of salvation is our impenetrable defense against anything the enemy throws at us. Jesus said, *Do not be afraid of those who kill the body but cannot kill the soul. Rather, be afraid of the One who can destroy both soul and body in hell* (Matthew 10:28). The idea in this verse is that, as we prepare for Satan's attacks, we must grab that helmet and buckle it on tightly. With this helmet of salvation, *We can destroy arguments and every lofty opinion raised against the knowledge of God, and take every thought captive to obey Christ* (2 Corinthians 10:5). When doubts creep in, lean into what you know you believe and hang tough! Our salvation has been fully secured by Jesus' death and resurrection.

6) The sword of the Spirit, which is the Word of God – *All Scripture is God-breathed and is useful for teaching, rebuking, correcting and training in*

righteousness (2 Timothy 3:16). Paul depicts God's Word as an offensive weapon in our spiritual arsenal which is used to not only thwart the attacks of the devil and his demons, but to conquer them. In boxing, a fighter may look good because of their ability to block their opponent's punches. But if they don't know how to throw punches they will not leave the ring victorious. The Sword of the Spirit is our offensive weapon to attack the enemy and push him away. This is why not only Scripture study, but Scripture memory is important. We can recall Scriptures we know by heart when we feel an impending attack.

7) Pray in the Spirit on all occasions – Praying in the Spirit means praying in sync with God's will and prompting. "Samuel Chadwick points out that the Holy Spirit never works alone—it is always in cooperation with men. He depends upon human cooperation for the mediation of His mind, the manifestation of His truth, and the effectual working of His will."[28] *Be alert and always keep on praying for all the Lord's people – be on your guard and stay awake. Your enemy, the devil, is like a roaring lion, sneaking around to find someone to attack* (1 Peter 5:8-9).

In Chapter eleven, we looked at the power of our stories to change hearts. Our testimonies serve another purpose as well. They inoculate us from the power of the Devil: *They triumphed over him (the devil) by the blood of the Lamb and by the word of their testimony; they did not love their lives so much as to shrink from death* (Revelation 12:11). Each one of us is a walking miracle! Recall to mind the amazing events and answers to prayer the Lord has used to draw you to himself. What personal experiences confirm for you that He is who He says He is? This is your unique story – stand on the truth of your testimony, Because It's All True!

Be Salty

God intends the most powerful of all restraints within sinful society to be his redeemed people. As R.V.G.Tasker says, God's disciples are "to be a moral disinfectant in a world where moral standards are low, constantly changing, or non-existent." [29]

Jesus said, *You are the salt of the earth. But if the salt loses its saltiness, how can it be made salty again? It is no longer good for anything, except to be thrown out and trampled underfoot* (Matthew 5:13). The effectiveness of salt is conditional: it must retain its saltiness. It can be watered-down or become contaminated by impurities, becoming useless; even dangerous.

To be effective the Christian must retain their Christlikeness, just as salt must retain its saltness. If Christians become assimilated with non-Christians and contaminated by the impurities of the world, thcy lose their influence. The influence of Christians in and on society depends on their being distinct, not identical. Dr. Lloyd-Jones emphasizes this: 'The glory of the gospel is that when the Church is absolutely different from the world, she invariably attracts it. It is then that the world is made to listen to her message, though it may hate it at first.' Otherwise if we Christians are indistinguishable from non-Christians, we are useless. We might as well be discarded like saltless salt, 'thrown out and trodden underfoot by men.'"[30]

Questions for Discussion

1. What is the Lord prompting you to stand up for or against right now?

2. With which parts of the spiritual armor are you most familiar? Which parts need to be applied more fully?

3. When spiritually attacked, how do you react? How should you?

4. What action will you put in My Plan for Thriving to better equip yourself for the spiritual battle?

CHAPTER 17

Is Walking Obediently Possible? Freedom Awaits!

Whoever has my commands and obeys them is the one who loves me. The one who loves me will be loved by my Father, and I too will love them and show myself to them.
John 14:21

My dear children, I write this to you so that you will not sin. But if anybody does sin, we have an advocate with the Father—Jesus Christ, the Righteous One.
1 John 2:1

What is true worship? It isn't just what we do in public but what we offer the Lord in private. When we resist temptation, we are worshipping him. When we put aside our agenda to help someone in need, that is worship too. As we strive to walk in obedience with Jesus, not constrained by regular habitual sin, we experience God-honoring worship. Moreover, we experience righteousness – we thrive!

Is sinlessness possible this side of heaven? Oh how I wish the answer were Yes, but it is not. We are imperfect people running after a perfect God. So, unblemished obedience is not the goal Scripture teaches. Walking with the desire of obedience ever before us, like frontlets on the foreheads of the early Hebrews, should be our aim. We should be growing in obedience as we grow in Christ because doing what He says honors the Lord and feels right in our gut. Righteousness is experienced when we are living as God intended.

R.C. Sproul offers this perspective: "We are unable to keep the Law perfectly and must rely upon Christ alone who has kept the Law perfectly and can alone put His people into right standing with God. Nevertheless, we must be concerned with obedience to God's commands, for in our obedience we show that we possess true saving faith."[31]

James 2:10 reminds us of the impossibility of perfectly following God's Law: "*For whoever keeps the whole law but fails in one point has become guilty of all of it.*" The law of God is one entity. We cannot excuse the breaking of a small portion of the commandments just because we are honoring the "Big" ones. That would be like an adulterer bragging that he has never stolen anything. They are still a lawbreaker! It is only by God's grace in paying the penalty for our imperfection on the cross that we can walk humbly in a relationship with the Lord.

But the one who looks into the perfect law, the law of liberty, and perseveres, being no hearer who forgets but a doer who acts, he will be blessed in his doing (James 1:25). Scripture tells us God's Word is perfect; therefore, it is exactly what we need. We were created to thrive when we walk in obedience to His Word. Paul refers to God's Word as the "Law of Liberty." We find freedom to be ourselves, unbound from the weight of sin and worldliness, when we walk in harmony with God.

Pastor Sam Allberry uses the illustration of a fish caught on a line and flopping on the deck of the fisherman's boat to show that a fish is only truly free when it is in the water. We humans are only free when we live within the constraints of God's law of liberty.[32]

When you get a D minus in 10th grade algebra it becomes a permanent stain on your academic record (believe me, I know!). Your grade point average will forever be less because of that poor grade. Thankfully, our Lord does not keep score the way teachers do. When we sin, we have an advocate willing to forgive that sin and expunge it entirely from our record. Listen to what the Apostle John said, *I am writing these things to you so that you may not sin. But if anyone does sin, we have an advocate with the Father, Jesus Christ the righteous* (1 John 2:1). Jesus' death on the cross was sufficient to cover ALL of our sins; past, present and future!

Here is some perspective on how Jesus wants us to handle sin as we strive for obedience. When Jesus approached Peter to wash his feet following the Last Supper, Peter asked, *'Lord, are you going to wash my feet?' Jesus replied, 'You do not realize now what I am doing, but later you will understand.' 'No,' said Peter, 'you shall never wash my feet!' Jesus answered, 'Unless I wash you, you have no part with me.' 'Then, Lord,' Simon Peter replied, 'not just my feet but my hands and my head as well!' Jesus answered, 'Those who have had a bath need only to wash their feet; their whole body is clean'* (John 13:6-10).

I think you see the point Jesus is reinforcing to Peter. Jesus was about to pay the price for Peter and all of our sins so we can be redeemed and walk with the Lord throughout our lives. When we stumble, we need only confess our misstep and we are forgiven. Catholic priests suggest a penance following a confession, and then pray a prayer of absolution, releasing the parishioner from their guilt. The journey with Jesus continues.

I heard a story years ago of when Billy Graham came to my fair city (Washington, DC) for a crusade back in the late 70s. A reporter interviewed Dr. Graham probing for any secrets as to his impeccable reputation and character in the face of so many evangelists who had fallen into sin. The reporter was hoping

Dr. Graham would reveal something profound like, "I wake up before I go to bed and pray for ten hours to start each day." But no, Billy's response was humble and succinct and went something like this: "I'm a sinner walking with a loving God. I practice confession and repentance daily so sin does not get a foothold in my life." Not only does that sound pretty simple, it also feels doable. What do you think?

The Relationship Between Answered Prayer and Obedience

W. Bingham Hunter writes, "Jesus taught that obedience and answered prayer are related: Jesus said, *If you abide in Me, and My words abide in you, ask whatever you wish, and it shall be done for you* (John 15:7). Abiding in Christ is sometimes explained in esoteric terms. But abiding is not mystical. It's primarily volitional: a matter of morality and ethics. Abiding is explained in 1 John 3:24: *The one who keeps His commandments abides in Him, and He in him.* Hence, the Apostle says: *...we have confidence before God; and whatever we ask we receive from him, because we keep his commandments and do what pleases him* (1 John 3:21-22)."[33]

It is important to note that there is no heavenly deal that says "You get answers to prayers to the same degree you obey." The prayer-obedience relationship is not a mechanized system but rather a fluid relationship. W. Bingham Hunter continues, "God is not a divine vending machine, into which we must place so many units of obedience before pulling the lever (through prayer) that causes answers to drop into our hands. The clay simply cannot control the hand of the Potter who works all things according to the counsel of his will (Ephesians 1:11).'

Does it seem fair that scripture says we receive from God when or because we obey him? Most families have rules they expect their children to follow based on what parents believe is best. If the kids are disobedient, do good parents simply dismiss their disobedience as if to say their rules weren't worth taking seriously? By no means! Disobedient children are not rewarded for bad behavior.

Prayer holds more power to change lives and change our world than any of the other tools in our arsenal.

Instead, they face discipline appropriate for their actions. Profoundly more than earthly parents, the Lord knows what is best for His children. This is why God yearns to draw us close – so that we better understand His ways, and can pray in accordance with His will. Disobedience takes us off course. Obedient following keeps us growing and living in harmony with God, ourselves, and our neighbors (at least most of the time!).

As we grow in Christ we learn to see life more through His eyes and gradually take on a Kingdom perspective. This perspective allows us to discern God's will more clearly, and thus enables us to pray more in keeping with His will. As we journey with Christ, we get more in tune with the Holy Spirit speaking to us from within (see chapter 20). When we pray for things not part of God's will, those prayers are not answered in the affirmative (though they are still answered – yes, no, not now are all answers). But when we pray according to God's will, as the Spirit prompts us, Scripture assures the potency of our prayers – *This is the confidence we have in approaching God: that if we ask anything according to his will, he hears us. And if we know that he hears us—whatever we ask—we know that we have what we asked of him* (1 John 5:14-15).

Prayer holds more power to change lives and change our world than any of the other tools in our arsenal. Yes, our love for one another, our incarnational presence in people's lives, our ability to speak and defend the faith, our stories, our service and sacrifice are all vital aspects of our witness. But none are equal to the power of prayer. That is why prayer should undergird each of these other activities of Christian service.

Scripture is clear that sin only has power over us to the extent we allow it to have power. Thankfully, Jesus has provided us with the means for victory – *No temptation has overtaken you except what is common to mankind. And God is faithful; he will not let you be tempted beyond what you can bear. But when you are tempted, he will also provide a way out so that you can endure it* (1 Corinthians 10:13).

It is easy over time to get used to certain sins just being a part of our makeup. The old saying, "Boys will be boys" plants the mindset that young men are destined to be troublemakers. We accept certain bad habits will continue to dog our feet rather than doing the work to take them down. Scripture promises that we are empowered by the Lord to break the chain of habitual sins. Listen to how David prayed – *Keep steady my steps according to your promise, and let no iniquity get dominion over me* (Psalm 119:133). In Christ we have been set free from habitual sin; it no longer needs to control us. Lean into His Spirit and trust Him to overcome!

Nearly every believer wants to be set free from regular sins that dog our feet. Willpower alone usually doesn't suffice. I suggest finding a close brother or sister, one of those covenant friends discussed earlier, and lay your soul bare before them. Ask them to be praying for you and to hold you accountable. Coming clean with your struggle fuels your path to victory.

In conclusion, there is a clear relationship between our efficacy in prayer and our commitment to do what Jesus says. In the Sermon on the Mount Jesus lays bare his listeners when He says, *Why do you call me, 'Lord, Lord,' and not do what I tell you* (Luke 6:46)? I don't hear this as a scolding but rather as a pleading because our Lord so desperately wants us to experience the thriving available to us, and to those we influence for His sake.

We have confidence before God and receive from him anything we ask, because we keep his commands and do what pleases him (1 John 3:21-22). *And, We know that God does not listen to sinners. He listens to the godly person who does his will* (John 9:31). So let's raise our standard in our commitment to live righteously before God and see if we don't connect with His heart in prayer more than we ever have before. *Consecrate yourselves, for tomorrow the Lord will do amazing things among you* (Joshua 3:5).

Questions to Consider

1. Where did you form your perspective on how much obedience is expected or possible?

2. Is there a regular habitual sin you would like to confess, both to God and to a friend, and move on from? Write in your calendar when you will take this step.

3. How are you feeling challenged to pray differently?

Chapter 18

Practice the Presence of God

He appointed twelve that they might be with him.
Mark 3:14

Yet I am always with you; you hold me by my right hand. You guide me with your counsel, and afterward you will take me into glory.
Psalm 73:23-24

As relatively new grandparents, Kris and I desperately want to be regular fixtures in our grandchildren's lives. Fortunately, one grandchild lives fairly close, but the others are a couple of hours away. However, it is nothing for us to drive four hours to watch a forty-five-minute soccer game or see a pre-school graduation. Just "being there" reaffirms our love and commitment to them, and warms our hearts at the same time.

Here's the point: If we imperfect grandparents are this enthralled with our offspring, how much more do you think our perfect heavenly father wants to involved in all that we do? It is hard to imagine a single aspect of our lives He wouldn't want to be invited to enjoy with us (see chapter 8 for more on this).

Psalm 37:23-24 says, *The Lord directs the steps of the godly. He delights in every detail of their lives. Though they stumble, they will never fall, for the Lord holds them by the hand.* Do you think He protects our stumbling only when we're in church? No! He walks with us through every moment of our day and is completely engaged with us! He yearns for our thriving in all that we do.

If the Lord's priority was only that we follow his directives he would have just written them down and been done with it. He would not have had to walk hundreds of miles with his disciples, sleep on rocky mountain slopes, and die a humiliating and painful death. Jesus wanted to be in the center of this journey with His disciples, and He desires the same for you and me today. Our relationship with Him is His highest priority. I have told thousands of teens over the years: "If you were the only person on earth, the story wouldn't have changed – Jesus Christ would have died for You!" – because he wants a personal relationship with us more than anything!

Joshua 1:9 says, t*he Lord is with you WHEREVER you go!* [emphasis added] What's included in "wherever?" R.C. Sproul, the founder of Ligonier Ministries, popularized the Latin phrase, Coram Deo, which simply means, "Living before the face of God." For some, this might be a frightening picture, as if God were a cruel judge waiting in the shadows to catch us when we're out of line. A truer picture of the God of the Bible is one who is standing with arms wide, like the Prodigal Father in the parable, to embrace us throughout the day, and to cheer us on to victory. Our 24/7 fellowship is His chief desire.

In Matthew 26 we see Jesus dining in the house of Simon the Leper. Most scholars conclude that Simon was one of the hundreds of people Jesus healed during His ministry – perhaps even the leper healed in Luke 5 when Jesus was still calling his first disciples. What do we learn about Jesus from this encounter?

One can imagine that Simon would feel like he had received a whole new lease on life after being healed of this dreadful disease, right? But a mere physical healing was not Jesus' only objective, nor was it enough for Simon. They both sought to be together in life. This scene exhibits Jesus' commitment to Simon's sanctification – He was concerned with Simon's heart and continued growth in Him on his journey toward heaven. Our God yearns to dine with us as well!

The Example of Brother Lawrence

In the 1600's, a monk named, Brother Lawrence, worked in the kitchen of a Carmelite monastery in Paris. He wrote a classic book titled, "The Practice of the Presence of God." It chronicles this brother's quest to acknowledge the presence of Jesus every waking moment of the day. While no one could perfectly fulfill this goal, Brother Lawrence came very close. Like many of us, Brother Lawrence likely began each day with some sort of devotional practice. But he didn't leave the Lord there at the altar. He abided with Jesus as he cooked, as he walked in nature, as he conversed with others. Brother Lawrence raised the bar for me in what is possible in my relationship with Jesus. I am challenged to reach higher than I've traveled before and to not limit God.

How might we practically acknowledge God's pleasure throughout each day?

Bookend the day in prayer. In the morning, pray through your day inviting Jesus to be with you in every part, and picturing what His presence might look like. Then, as you put your head on the pillow at night, reflect thankfully on how the Lord showed up during the day. Our Catholic brethren call this evening prayer, the Examen, a time to thank the Lord for where we saw Him during the day, to confess where we strayed from him, and to reaffirm our desire to be all his.

Another way to experience the presence of the Lord is to walk as a witness always on the lookout for opportunities for our faith to impact the people we encounter. Since sharing our faith is intimidating for most of us, this process draws us to depend on the Holy Spirit for strength. We can't, nor would we want to go about witnessing without Him!

Finally, practice thanking God throughout each day. Look for the good things His presence brings to mind, rather than focusing on the trials of the day. Paul's instruction to the Philippians is so important for us: *Do not be anxious about anything, but in every situation, by prayer and petition, <u>with thanksgiving</u>, present your requests to God. And the peace of God, which transcends all understanding, will guard your hearts and your minds in Christ Jesus* (Philippians 4:6-7). In which situations does the Lord want us to petition Him? That's right, every one of them! So how much of our lives is He interested in? ALL OF IT!!! We never need to feel alone because we never are!

Questions to Consider

1. Describe how much the Lord desires intimate fellowship with you. How are you doing at receiving this gift He offers?

2. What could you do to invite or envision the Lord with you during the various aspects of your day? Transfer these steps to My Plan for Thriving.

Chapter 19

Is the Sabbath a Command or a Suggestion?

If you turn back your foot from the Sabbath, from doing your pleasure on my holy day, and call the Sabbath a delight and the holy day of the Lord honorable; if you honor it, not going your own ways, or seeking your own pleasure, or talking idly; then you shall take delight in the Lord, and I will make you ride on the heights of the earth .
Isaiah 58:13-14a

There is so much written on the command of a Sabbath day of rest that I will only touch on it here briefly. My responses to the following questions are not meant to satisfy your seeking, but to stimulate more of it…

1. What was the original command regarding the Sabbath, and what did it mean to the original audience?

2. What light does the New Testament shed on how to honor the Sabbath today?

3. Who is the Sabbath for; us or God?

4. What are the benefits to observing this command, and what are the costs not to?

Keeping the Sabbath is not only one of the "Big Ten" commandments – it is also the one with the most description regarding how to live it out and why. The ancient Hebrews religiously observed a weekly sabbath where they reminded themselves that God was holy and supreme, and they were finite. They fully rested during that twenty-four-hour period. Rest and Worship were their two priorities. Let's look at this commandment from Deuteronomy 5 line by line looking for insights for our edification:

- *Observe the Sabbath day, to keep it holy, as the Lord your God commanded you* (Deuteronomy 5:12). Is the Sabbath a suggestion or a command? It's a command. Now, what does it mean to observe the Sabbath day?

- *Six days you shall labor and do all your work, but the seventh day is a Sabbath to the Lord your God. On it you shall not do any work* (Exodus 20:9-10)... *And, By the seventh day God had finished the work He had been doing; so on the seventh day He rested from all His work* (Genesis 2:2). We have six days to fill anyway we would like. The Lord desires to be with us in all those activities as we already discussed. However, the seventh day is a day not to work or do what we want. It is a day given to the Lord. It is a day where our weekly rhythms change dramatically. The result should be rest for us, and honor to God. So how do we give God the honor He is due?

- *...you or your son or your daughter or your male servant or your female servant, or your ox or your donkey or any of your livestock, or the sojourner who is within your gates, that your male servant and your female servant may rest as well as you* (Deuteronomy 5:14). The Sabbath is intended to be a community experience. If some are working and others are not, it makes things a bit more challenging. Bravo Chick Fil-A!

- You shall remember that you were a slave in the land of Egypt, and the Lord your God brought you out from there with a mighty hand and an outstretched arm. Therefore, the Lord your God commanded you to keep the Sabbath day (Deuteronomy 5:15). The key word here is "Remember." The Sabbath is a day to remind us of God's faithfulness to us, and to all mankind, all the way back to the Creation account. Recounting God's mighty deeds strengthens our faith in Him and fuels our resolve to remain true at all times. *I will remember the deeds of the Lord; yes, I will remember your wonders of old. I will ponder all your work, and meditate on your mighty deeds* (Psalm 77:11-12).

Pastor Caleb Mathis of Crossroads church in Cincinnati beautifully compares the Sabbath to a snow day: "Remember the excitement of a snow day? Getting up early to check the TV scroll. Your school is listed! You jump back in bed and sleep as late as you want. When you wake up, an entire day waits for you, a blank canvas on which to craft a masterpiece. That's Sabbath—a holy snow day. And God gives us 52 of them a year!"

So who was the Sabbath made for – us or God? Jesus answered this question quite plainly: The sabbath was made for man, and not man for the sabbath (Mark 2:27). The Sabbath was intended to be a gift from God to us; to help us be healthy and balanced. It should not feel like a burden but a welcome hiatus in our week.

Clearly, God's people are called to rest one day a week from their ordinary employment. This applies to folks in the workforce as well as to pastors and Christian workers. Just because they are involved in "God's work" doesn't disqualify them from the need for a Sabbath. Moses commanded the workmen building the tabernacle to observe a day of rest. So should we. Not everyone can observe their Sabbath on the same day. We need emergency personnel on call, and pastors are certainly at work on Sundays. These folks are free to choose a different day of the week to rest that fits their schedule.

Paul wrote this to the young church in Colossae: *Therefore let no one pass judgment on you in questions of food and drink, or with regard to a festival or a new moon or a Sabbath. These are a shadow of the things to come, but the substance belongs to Christ. If with Christ you died to the elemental spirits of the world, why, as if you were still alive in the world, do you submit to regulations—Do not handle, Do not taste, Do not touch (referring to things that perish as they are used)—according to human precepts and teachings* (Colossians 2:16-17; 20-22)?

Remember, Jesus *is Lord of the Sabbath* (Matthew 12:8). This agrees with much of the New Testament teaching that God does not desire legalism or ritualistic observances. He wants our hearts. Jesus does not want the Sabbath to be a burden but a joy. However, the priorities of worship and rest remain a useful prism for designing our Sabbath today.

Through the centuries the Jewish people added more and more rules to help people religiously observe the Sabbath. It got to the point where they could almost do nothing but worship and sit at home. Jesus saw their plight and used an object lesson to instruct His Pharisaical listeners: *He went on from there and entered their synagogue. And a man was there with a withered hand. And they asked him, 'Is it lawful to heal on the Sabbath?'—so that they might accuse him. He said to them, 'Which one of you who has a sheep, if it falls into a pit on the Sabbath, will not take hold of it and lift it out? Of how much more value is a man than a sheep! So it is lawful to do good on the Sabbath.' Then he said to the man, 'Stretch out your hand.' And the man stretched it out, and it was restored, healthy like the other* (Matthew 12:9-13).

It is important to note that Jesus did not abolish any part of the Law; He came to fulfill the Law. His words did not nullify the command to practice a Sabbath day's rest. He challenged the rules the religious leaders had piled onto the original command; not the command itself. *God is not a man that he should lie, or a son of man that he should change his mind* (Numbers 23:19).

What is Expected of our Sabbath Observances?

Church attendance has historically been a widely accepted component of sabbath observance. However, forty million Americans have stopped attending church since the year 2000. That's about 12 percent of the population, and it represents the largest concentrated change in church attendance in American history.[34] No wonder chaos is on the rise and morality is being shelved. *The fool says in his heart, 'There is no God.' They are corrupt, they do abominable deeds; there is none who does good* (Psalm 14:1). Could the failure of the vast majority of us to honor the Sabbath be contributing to our societal missteps?

D.L. Moody poignantly illustrates our societal and individual neglect of the Sabbath with this story…

> Suppose, again, that one man was met on a road by another man to whom he gave six dollars, and kept only one dollar for himself to pay his expenses to the end of the journey. Suppose the other turned on him, knocked him down, and took away his one dollar. Would not his ingratitude arouse our indignation? Yet God gifted us six days to spend as we desire and ordained one where we would take time to worship him corporately. Why do we so easily rob him of that day?[35]

Sin takes no Sabbath, nor should acts of charity.

Jesus healed on the Sabbath. Was this breaking the command? Certainly not! No, Jesus showed these legalistic pharisees that acts of mercy and service on the Sabbath are not only acceptable, but encouraged. Sin takes no Sabbath, nor should acts of charity.

John Mark Comer speaks of the Sabbath not as one day but rather a rhythm for how to live the entire week. "The Sabbath isn't just a twenty-four-hour time slot in in your weekly schedule; it's a spirit of restfulness that goes with us throughout our week. A way of living with ease, gratitude, appreciation, peace and prayer. A way of working from rest, not for rest, with nothing to prove. A way of bearing fruit from abiding, not ambition."[36] The days leading up to the Sabbath are preparation for what comes on the Sabbath. What chores can we get done during the week so that we are ready to rest and worship?

Allow me to repeat the opening verse of this chapter. Through the prophet Isaiah the Lord gave this exhortation to His people: *If you turn back your foot from the Sabbath, from doing your pleasure on my holy day, and call the Sabbath a delight and the holy day of the Lord honorable; if you honor it, not going your own ways, or seeking your own pleasure, or talking idly; then you shall take delight in the Lord, and I will make you ride on the heights of the earth; I will feed you with the heritage of Jacob your father, for the mouth of the Lord has spoken* (Isaiah 58:13-14). Riding on the heights of the earth sounds like thriving to me!

To sum up, here is a very short list of suggestions

TO DO and TO AVOID on the Sabbath:

TO DO

Worship God

Remember God's faithful deeds

Rest

Read the Bible and pray

Visit with family and friends

Walk, hike or ride a bike

Serve a neighbor or shut-in

Plan a fun family activity

Lead a family devotional

Attend church

TO AVOID

Tasks associated with our job

Labor that drains rather than refreshes (yardwork!!!)

Participating in activities that cause others to work

Errands and chores

Being connected to your phone all day

Preparing burdensome meals

Anything that causes stress more than rest

*Watching or playing sports? (you decide)

What are the Consequences of Ignoring the Sabbath?

In creation, God established a rhythm for thriving – it is six days on and one off. We thrive when we participate in this rhythm, and we struggle when we buck it. Look at the health crisis caused by workaholism. And look at the societal decay caused by the moral decline as a result of decreased church attendance and belief in God. We are not winning by ignoring the Sabbath.

Missy Takano sums this up well: "Sabbath is not a commandment we are bound to; it's a promise we're invited to enjoy. Sabbath rest is an invitation to practice for eternity in God's presence. It is an act of regular and intentional trust of God's rule on Earth. When we stop working, we can truly rest in God's presence. When we practice this purposeful pause, we make room for God to take up residence in our individual lives and communities. And when we do this, we take part in the new creation story, setting the stage for God to make his dwelling place once again on Earth."[37] We are free from the Mosaic Law and instead under the law of Christ, which is to love God with all of our being and to love our neighbors as we love ourselves.

Whenever we stray from God's will we experience hardship and distance in our relationship with Jesus. There is a correlation between obedience and intimate fellowship, just as we discussed the correlation between obedience and answered prayer in chapter 17. When we fail to honor the Sabbath, we miss out on the goodness offered us by our gracious Lord. Because it's all true!

Questions to Consider

1. What does your current practice of the Sabbath look like? What is good, and what might you be missing?

2. What do you find difficult about honoring the Sabbath?

3. What could a more faithful observance of a Sabbath do for you? How might you (and your family) benefit?

4. What step(s) will you add to My Plan for Thriving to more faithfully honor the Sabbath?

CHAPTER 20

Learn to Discern God's Voice Speaking to You

By Pastor Rick Reiter

Rick Reiter is pastor and founder of Come Close Ministries. He is known for his ability to make biblical teachings accessible and to help beievers better connect with the voice of God. Rick has a Masters of Divinity from Multnomah Biblical Seminary, where he was awardded the Faculty Award for Spiritual Life. It is a blessing for him to share his wisdom with us.

When we talk about hearing God's voice, there are two main vehicles God uses to share His heart, thoughts, insights, wisdom, direction, ways, and more. The Bible, which are the very words of God, and the Holy Spirit, God's very presence in the heart of every believer. When we learn how to engage the Word and the Spirit hearing God becomes simpler and a part of our everyday life.

God tells us that the Bible is not just some book filled with ancient thoughts, stories, and wisdom. It's something much greater than that – it is the very words of God. Every word, every thought, every story is a word that God has breathed (2 Timothy 3:16-17). The book of Hebrews tells us that God's Word is alive and active. When we open our Bible, we're experiencing the heart of God, the wisdom of God, the ways of God, so His Word is actively at work in our heart to connect us with His heart.

The Bible is not intended to merely be studied academically; it is God's love letter to us. It's God reaching down from Heaven to touch our hearts, minds, bodies, and souls with His heart and truth. It's His pursuit of us, a declaration of His love for us, an invitation to be in relationship with Him, a revelation of His character, majesty, and so much more. This is why we approach Scripture with open hearts, expecting to be met, loved, and shaped by the God who speaks through it.

How do we approach God's Word relationally, rather than just academically? When we study it academically, we engage the mind; when we approach the Bible relationally, we engage the heart. Ideally, we want to engage both the heart and the mind. There are many great resources out there for how to engage the Bible with our mind, but in this chapter, I'm going to focus on the relational side – how to engage with our heart so as to hear His heart.

To engage the heart, we need a posture the Bible calls "The fear of God." No, that does not mean to be afraid of God – quite the opposite – it means to be in awe of God, to love and respect God in a way that takes your breath away. It's an awe that says you're the most amazing thing in the entire world, you alone have infinite wisdom, love, power, majesty, compassion, and more. It's with this attitude that the heart seeks God. It is displayed in the way we approach God and His Word, how we receive His Presence and His Word in our lives, and how we respond to His truth and His gentle corrections about how to live. It is seen in

When we approach God with this sort of awe, with a posture of healthy fear – we position ourselves to hear Him speak.

our loving obedient response to His ways. It is visible in our worship – the expression of thanks and praise to all that He is. When we approach God with this sort of awe, with a posture of healthy fear – we position ourselves to hear Him speak.

Proverbs 2 gives us great insight as to what it means to fear God. In this passage we learn five ways to engage God and His Word so that we gain His presence, wisdom, leading, and heart.

> My son, if you accept my words
> and store up my commands within you,
> turning your ear to wisdom
> and applying your heart to understanding—
> indeed, if you call out for insight
> and cry aloud for understanding,
> and if you look for it as for silver
> and search for it as for hidden treasure,
> then you will understand the fear of the LORD
> and find the knowledge of God (Proverbs 2:1-5).

Here are the five important attitudes of the heart needed to hear God's voice in our lives:

1. Accept God's words
2. Store up His commands
3. Apply our hearts to understanding
4. Call out for insight & cry aloud for understanding
5. Look for Him as one looking for silver or hidden treasure

What follows is a practical way to approach God and His Word to help us fear Him, find Him, and hear His voice.

First, before opening the Word of God, pray and connect with Him. Thank Him that you get to spend time with Him. Thank Him that He has taken the time to make Himself known to you through His Word. Welcome Him into this moment. Tell Him that you want to see His heart, character, and ways as you sit with His Word. Ask Him to give you a heart that is soft and sensitive to Him; one that accepts what He has to say. Ask Him to help you internalize and store up His truths and ways. Ask Him to teach you and give you divine understanding. Finally, ask him to show you the hidden things He reserves for those who love him.

Now, let's unpack the attitudes that are reflected in that opening prayer that spring from Proverbs 2.

1. Accept God's Words

God tells us that if we fear Him, we will accept His words. To accept God's words means to receive them as true, even if what God says is contrary to what the world says about life, love, or the pursuit of happiness. God's ways are often contrary to the ways of the world. It often is contrary to the way we have lived our lives. When we read the Bible, if we have an attitude that says, "I receive what you say as true," we put our hearts in a position to "hear" what God has to say to us.

Proverbs 1:23 tells us that when we listen and respond to God's voice, He pours out His thoughts to us. In other words, God is looking for a posture that says, "Lord, whatever You say, I will receive as truth—and I will respond to it." When we come to Him this way, He graciously pours His wisdom into us and reveals the treasures of His heart that He reserves for those who seek Him with openness and surrender. So, the first attitude is to be ready to accept His Word as truth in our lives.

2. Store Up His Commands

The second attitude is to have a willing heart to store up God's commands.

In life, we store up many things. We store up money in the form of savings accounts. We store up food in our pantries and freezers. We store up vacation days at work so we can get away to the beach. We store anything we consider valuable or necessary.

When do we actually store things up? We don't store them when we need them; we store them ahead of time so they are available when a need arises. We must trust that when we open the Word of God, He will give us what is necessary and valuable for our lives. Even if it doesn't seem like a text is applicable in that moment, we say, "Thank you, God, for revealing that truth to me. I'll store this away for later when I need it." When we store up God's Word, we internalize it, storing it in our hearts so it is available when a timely moment arises.

When I was a teenager reading the Bible, God showed me many things about marriage. I didn't need them at the time, but I "stored them up" in my heart. When the time came, His truth was in me, and I was able to recall those truths and apply them to my marriage. If we are in awe of Him, love Him, worship Him… "fear Him", we'll store up His truth, trusting Him as the one who leads us, not only in this moment, but in moments to come.

How do we store up God's word? We take the time to meditate on God's Word and memorize it. This is what puts His Word in our hearts so it's there when we need it.

3. Apply our Hearts to Understanding

When we seek only to understand the Word of God, we gain head knowledge. When we seek to apply His truth to our lives, we gain heart knowledge. It is one thing to know about God; it is an entirely different thing to "know God." To truly know God is to take what He reveals about Himself and allow those truths to shape the way we live. For example, if Scripture tells us that "a gentle answer turns away wrath," then we respond to others with gentleness when they are angry with us. And if He invites us to cast all our anxiety on Him, then we intentionally bring our worries to Him, trusting that He cares. In living this way, His Word becomes part of our daily rhythm, and our relationship with Him deepens.

Psalm 119:105 says that God's Word *"is a lamp unto our feet and a light unto our path."* God's Word is like a flashlight, allowing us to see, not the end of the path, but enough of it to navigate our next steps. When we step into what we see, more of the path is illuminated, and we then see the next step to take.

If you want to hear God in your life, step into what He has already revealed to you. This is applying God's Word! When you step into what you know, you're putting yourself in a position where God can reveal more to you. Some of us feel like we don't hear God, because we are waiting for the "whole picture". God often invites us to trust Him one or two steps at a time. Applying what we know is taking a step into what God has revealed. In your quiet time with Jesus, ask Him to show you how to live out what you've read as you move through your day. You'll find His Spirit gently nudging and reminding you at just the right moments—and in those gentle promptings, you'll be hearing God speak to you.

4. Call out for Insight and Cry Aloud for Understanding

Have you ever read God's Word and wondered, "What did I just read?" I have! Have you ever felt confused and not sure where to turn? Sometimes God's Word holds a truth that isn't seen right away. It is reserved for those who truly seek Him. Proverbs 2 implores us to cry out to God for understanding and insight.

This picture of crying out was best described by my friend Tom Donovan. He likened it to a baby who is crying for food. When a baby cries for food, it's not a whimper, it's not a soft request; it is a full-body experience. Their body tenses, and they scream out for what they need. God yearns for us to cry out to Him to lead us, direct us, and give us insight. The crying out can look like someone on their knees praying to God for help. It can look like consistent prayer. It can look like setting aside significant time to go and be alone with the Lord and seek His face. It can look like fasting for a season. It can take on many forms, but at its heart it is a demonstration from us that we need Him, and yearn for Him to speak to us.

We want to involve God in every aspect of our lives. Crying out to Him is the way to access God's leading, direction, wisdom, provision, and more. As I wrote this chapter, I didn't want you to receive my thoughts, I wanted God's help. I had written a few different drafts and none of them seemed right. I even had a completed draft that was all ready to send and my computer lost the file. Through all of this, I had the sense that my approach wasn't fully what God desired – so I cried out to Him for direction. After two days of fasting, I sat down at my computer and, in a complete stream of consciousness, wrote this chapter. It just flowed. Why? I believe it is because I cried out to God for His help. So let me gently ask you: Where do you need to cry out to Him? In what area do you need His wisdom or His nearness? What burden or confusion do you need to bring before Him? Whatever it is, cry out to God—He has what your heart needs.

When we come before God with humility and ask, "Lord, give me insight. Show me how this truth becomes life in me,"

He responds. At times, the application feels clear and effortless. Other times, it is formed through tears, persistence, and a deep longing for His help. Yet, in every season, His Spirit gently leads us into a deeper understanding.

5. Look for Him as One Looking for Silver or Hidden Treasure

Have you ever looked for silver or hidden treasure? When someone searches for silver, they go to a mine and dig through dirt in hopes of finding this valuable metal. Miners are likely to find nothing but dirt for hours, days, weeks, or even months. But they keep on digging. Why? Because they know silver is in there and well worth their effort to find it.

Seeking God can feel like that. God says that when we have the attitude of a miner, we will find Him (Mathew 6:33). When we feel like we haven't found what we're looking for, we keep digging because we know He has something valuable for us. Don't lose heart as you listen for God's whisper in His Word. If today's time in the Bible felt empty, stay with Him. Keep going, keep digging, keep believing that God has a nugget for you from His heart to yours.

People ask me all the time, "How do you hear God?" I honestly think it springs from continuing to seek His face EVEN when it felt dry. I've tried to apply what I know of Him and His Word to my life, I've cried out to Him when I didn't understand, and as a result, He has poured knowledge of Himself, and His ways, into my heart.

I've experienced the whisper of God's Spirit as He has brought scripture to my mind at just the right moment. He's dropped wisdom into my heart when I've asked Him what to do in a situation. I've had him teach me deep truths when I've asked, "What does this verse mean?" I've treated my quiet times like a relationship and saw my time in the Word of God not as an experience with a book but an experience with the living God.

There have been times when a particular Scripture kept finding its way to me—from a friend's text, a sermon, or an unexpected conversation. Eventually, I paused and asked, "Lord, what are You trying to show me through this verse?" In moments like that, I'm learning to recognize His voice as He brings His Word to my attention through many different pathways. And when I turn to Him and ask for understanding, He often brings gentle thoughts to mind that shed light on what He wants me to see. The insights He gives run deeper than anything I could discover on my own, and my walk with Jesus has grown richer as a result.

These five attitudes shape a heart that is ready to hear God. This is the posture of "fearing the Lord," and Proverbs 2 tells us that when we fear Him, we will discover the knowledge of God (v. 5) and His wisdom will enter our hearts (v. 10). That wisdom comes as a gentle, quiet voice—His Spirit whispering to our spirit about who He is and how He invites us to live.

Psalm 25:14 says that God *"confides in those who fear Him."* Confides is a powerful word; it means that God reveals the secrets of His heart to those who fear Him. To understand confiding I want you to think about connecting with one of your closest friends. Maybe you're in a coffee shop catching up, and the conversation moves from small talk to something deeper. When you notice no one is listening, you lean in closer to your friend and ask, "Can I tell you something?" You lower your voice so only they can hear, and you start to share the depths of your heart. This is confiding – when we tell the secrets of our heart to those closest to us in a way that others can't hear. To those who fear Him, God lays His heart bare and shows us secrets of His heart that He reserves just for His closest friends.

Confiding happens throughout the Scriptures. God leaned into Noah and said, "Noah, can I tell you something? I'm going to flood the world, build a boat." God appeared to Moses and said, "Moses, can I tell you something? I'm going to free the Israelites, go back to Egypt." God revealed His heart to Peter in a vision of a sheet and told him that the Gentiles were loved by God and offered His salvation as well. All through scripture God confides in those who fear Him, and often times through that confiding He is inviting those close to His heart to join Him in what He is doing.

I've had many moments in my life where I believe the Lord confided in me. It is these moments where God whispered His thoughts into my heart that I stepped into them and saw Him do big things. These are the stories that people love and why people ask me how I hear God – because they want to hear God like that. Here is one of those stories…

One night after a movie, my friend Tommy and I were driving home on windy country roads. He was enjoying his sports car, and I followed behind in my not so fancy, nor so sporty Mazda. Eventually, we got to his street, but he kept driving because he was having so much fun. We parted ways.

A few minutes later, I sensed the Lord whisper in my spirit, "Turn around. There's a serious accident on Hunter Mill Road." It wasn't audible—just a quiet, persistent impression I couldn't shake. Part of me wondered if it was simply worry, but the feeling remained strong. So I asked myself, What will it cost me to find out if this is God? The answer, was just fifty cents. I turned around, paid the extra fifty cent toll and headed back to where I came from to see if this was God speaking to me.

As I drove back down that dark, twisting road, concern for Tommy rose in my heart. And then, as I came over a hill, I saw it: smoke drifting through my headlights, debris scattered across the pavement, skid marks slicing across the road. I slowed down and there was a shadowy figure walking towards me. It was Tommy. As he approached my car, I rolled down my window and we both asked, "what are you doing here?"

My friend was safe, he wasn't in the accident, but the scene puzzled us both. Just moments before we drove this road and there was not an accident on it. But now, just 5 minutes later, there's debris from a horrible accident all over the road and a car off to the side that is dented, gnarled, windshield bashed in, but not a person to be found in it.

To anyone else, it would have appeared old and already handled. But we knew better. As we tried to figure out what happened, we heard faint, muffled cries coming from the woods. Following the sound, we found a woman lying in the darkness, badly injured and unable to move. We called 911, stayed with her, and made sure help arrived. Driving home that night, my heart was full. I knew—without question—that God had spoken. And I was humbled that He allowed us to take part in His rescue. But God wasn't finished…

A few weeks later, the woman called Tommy. She had found his number through the police report and hoped he could fill in the gaps of that night. After answering her questions, Tommy gently said, "Can I tell you something you haven't asked? You never asked how we found you." He continued, "My friend had already left the area. But God told him to turn around because there was a serious accident on Hunter Mill Road. God knew you were hurting. He knew you needed to be found. You matter to Him."

Tommy shared the gospel with her. We don't know how her story with God unfolded after that call. But we do know this: God sees. God speaks. God leads. And sometimes, by His grace, He invites us to join Him in what He is doing.

This was one of those sacred moments when I sensed God confiding in me. Why would He do that? First, because He cared deeply for the woman who needed to be found. And second, because I have sought—however imperfectly—to live as one who fears the Lord. Psalm 25:14 tells us that God confides in those who fear Him, and I believe He longs to do this with you and me. So often His gentle promptings are easy to overlook or dismiss, yet they may be His invitation to join Him in what He is doing. All it cost me that night was a small inconvenience—fifty cents and a willingness to turn around. But in taking that small step, I learned to recognize His voice.

My encouragement to you is this: walk in the fear of the Lord, expecting that Jesus is relational and near. When He reveals something—even in a whisper—step toward it with an open heart, and He will show you if it really was Him or not.

All of this points to an essential truth: the same God who speaks through Scripture also speaks to our hearts by His Spirit.

The Holy Spirit

As incredible as the gift of Scripture is, it was never meant to stand alone. The Bible teaches us who God is, reveals His truth, anchors us, and shapes our understanding — but God, in His kindness, went even further. Through His Word we learn who He is, and through His Spirit we come to know Him personally — not as a distant truth, but as a present and intimate companion.

God didn't just give us a book; He gave us Himself. The Holy Spirit is a gift that is even greater than His God-breathed Word; it is His very presence with us at all times. God speaks to our spirit by His Spirit. When God gave believers in Jesus the gift of the Holy Spirit, He gave us the ability to know the thoughts of God.

1 Corinthians 2:11-12 tells us: *For who knows a person's thoughts except their own spirit within them? In the same way no one knows the thoughts of God except the Spirit of God. What we have received is not the spirit of the world, but the Spirit who is from God, so that we may understand what God has freely given us.*

Did you know that we can know God's thoughts? That's exactly what this verse tells us. Because we have His Spirit, we can know the mind of God. Let that sink in! You and I have the Word of God, which is His very words breathed by Him into written form, and we have the Holy Spirit, who knows the mind of God and can reveal the mind of God to us personally.

This gift of the Holy Spirit is so amazing that Jesus said it was better for Him to leave His disciples and go be with the Father so He could send the Spirit to be with us all the time. This gift means that God is not with us only when we are at church, or reading our Bible, or doing something we deem to be "religious." God is with us in every capacity, and is always available to reveal His heart and mind.

Paul encourages us to pray without ceasing; to walk with an awareness of the Holy Spirit's presence at all times. As we acknowledge His presence in quiet conversation throughout the day, He will lead us with His thoughts. John 14:25-26 tells us the Holy Spirit will teach us all things, and remind us of everything Jesus has taught. When we engage the Holy Spirit as our teacher, we invite Him to:

- Teach us the Scriptures we don't understand
- Show us how to apply the truths of scripture to our daily lives
- Show us how He would respond to circumstances, people, and situations so we might do likewise

The Holy Spirit is a teacher. If we engage Him like a teacher, we will hear Him speak into our spirit with His thoughts, ways, and understanding. Likewise, the Holy Spirit reminds us of things God has taught us. When a scripture pops into our minds at the right moment, or we recall a Biblical principle, that is the Holy Spirit speaking to us.

The Holy Spirit is actively engaging us, speaking to us, leading us, and revealing God's heart to us. The Holy Spirit:

1. Teaches us

2. Reminds us of what God has revealed to us

3. Reveals our sin but lovingly invites us to repent and walk in His ways

4. Guides us into truth

5. Speaks to us what He hears God the Father and God the Son saying

6. Tells us things that are yet to come

7. Glorifies Jesus and the Father by making known what Jesus and the Father are saying

God is speaking to us all the time through the Word and through the Holy Spirit. When people say they can't hear God it is not because God isn't speaking; it's because people don't know how to tune in.

Here's one last example from everyday life. In your car, you probably have a radio. If you were to tune your radio to a certain station you would hear sounds that you couldn't hear before. Those sounds were bouncing all around you, but you couldn't hear them because you weren't tuned to their frequency. God's voice is like that. It's not that it's not present, it's that we don't know how to tune in to His still small voice. Once we learn how to tune into the Holy Spirit, we'll learn how to hear God's voice in our lives.

Questions to Consider

1. What experiences have you had with hearing God speak to you? Are you able to distinguish His voice from other competing voices?

2. What are some of your obstacles to hearing God?

3. What steps do you feel led to take to help learn to hear God speak to you in a personal way? (Note these in My Plan for Thriving)

A Free Gift from Rick Reiter

If you'd like to learn how to begin to tune into His voice I want to offer you a free gift. On my website I have a short training on how to discover God's voice in your life. In that short lesson I'll show you how God has been speaking to you your whole life and then show you how you can begin to tune into Him. You can find that short video resource here:

Here's the link to the suggested page:

https://www.comecloseministries.org/Because-Its-All-True

CHAPTER 21

Prepare to Endure Persecution

In fact, everyone who wants to live a godly life in Christ Jesus will be persecuted.
2 Timothy 3:12

Count it all joy, my brothers, when you meet trials of various kinds, for you know that the testing of your faith produces steadfastness. And let steadfastness have its full effect, that you may be perfect and complete, lacking in nothing.
James 1:2-4

I have said these things to you, that in me you may have peace. In the world you will have tribulation. But take heart; I have overcome the world.
John 16:33

Get on Offense

Yes, those of us who stand up to be counted as one of Christ's own will be persecuted; not always, but on occasion. Too often when we feel attacked for our faith we retreat. But we are not ashamed of the gospel (Jesus) because *...it is the power of God that brings salvation to everyone who believes...* (Romans 1:16). It's time to get on offense rather than play defense.

We must *Always be prepared to give an answer to everyone who asks you to give the reason for the hope that you have. But do this with gentleness and respect, keeping a clear conscience, so that those who speak maliciously against your good behavior in Christ may be ashamed of their slander. For it is better, if it is God's will, to suffer for doing good than for doing evil* (1 Peter 3:15-17). Adhering to the apostle's word here means standing firm upon what we believe is true; namely…

- We are proud to be counted as one of Christ's adopted sons or daughters; therefore, we proclaim this joyfully!
- We believe God's Word and the gospel is the best news anyone could hear; therefore, we unashamedly share it when given opportunity.
- We seek to turn ridicule into healthy dialogue while showing love to our persecutors. This helps them see Jesus in us.
- We experience God's favor and thriving when we say "Yes" to Him, rather than bowing to the world.

Religious persecution is rampant around the world but only more recently began rearing its ugly head here in America. People are being locked up or sued for expressing their faith by protesting at abortion clinics, or declining to participate in girls sporting events against transgender men. Statements of faith in Jesus are omitted from transcripts following interviews with prominent personalities. Christians who take a public stand on controversial issues risk being censored or canceled from social media. Whether you agree with their positions isn't the point. What is interesting is that just a generation ago these issues would have been unheard of.

No one desires to be persecuted for anything in which they are involved. But what an honor that we would take heat because of our allegiance to Jesus. *Blessed are those who are persecuted for righteousness' sake, for theirs is the kingdom of heaven. Blessed are you when others revile you and persecute you and utter all kinds of evil against you falsely on my account. Rejoice and be glad, for your reward is great in heaven, for so they persecuted the prophets who were before you* (Matthew 5:10-12).

In January of 2024, a Pew Research study found that 28% of Americans now identify as religiously unaffiliated, making them the largest single religious group in the U.S. In 2007 that group only comprised 16% of the population. The number of atheists within that percentage has doubled in just the past ten years, as has the number of agnostics. According to a Marist poll, only 31% of 18-29-year-olds believe in the God of the Bible. The bottom line is that for the first time in American history, we are living in an increasingly post-Christian nation.

How Did We Get Here?

How did this happen? For many years the Church has tried to straddle the line between standing for Scriptural truth and being culturally relevant. Some denominations changed their doctrinal statements to appeal to the changing morals of society. Most of these have lost rather than gained adherents.

John Mark Comer says the problem in the West is "…we have created a cultural milieu where you can be a Christian but not an apprentice to Jesus."[38] The daily focus for ancient rabbinical apprentices was to be with their master, become like their master, and imitate the activity of their master. This was the aim of their existence. In contrast, today many people raise their hand or pray a prayer of commitment to Jesus but are not told ahead of time that following Him will be costly (and not always popular) – and that the Lord instructed any would-be disciple to...*deny themselves, take up their cross daily and follow Me* (Luke 9:23).

Who is Behind the Secularization of America?

Our country was founded on Judeo-Christian values. The Bible is the most quoted book by our founding fathers. Biblical values were embraced as mainstays in American culture as the vast majority of Americans were devout church goers. Until the 1960's, 98% of Americans believed in God.

What and who has led to the recent surge of secularization in America? Many point to educational elites infiltrating our institutions of learning and indoctrinating the next generation with progressive ideas. The riots on campuses surrounding the conflict between Hamas and Israel is a recent example. The film and music industry have also been leading influencers of what is cool, and trendy. Social media has a very strong secular bent as algorithms govern what messages are allowed the most travel (and which ones are blocked). What motivates these institutions to want to significantly alter our moral fiber? For those familiar with the teachings of the Bible there is a clear author behind this effort.

Jesus calls out the source of those who reject God's Word and His teachings: *You belong to your father, the devil, and you want to carry out your father's desires. He was a murderer from the beginning, not holding to the truth, for there is no truth in him. When he lies, he speaks his native language, for he is a liar and the father of lies. Yet because I tell the truth, you do not believe me! Whoever belongs to God hears what God says. The reason you do not hear is that you do not belong to God* (John 8:42-45,47).

There is no truth in him… The devil entices people to sin, making evil seem appealing so that people choose evil over obedience to God (see James 1:14). His aim is to entice believers to marginalize Jesus and keep them from the fulfillment of their ultimate purpose to bring glory to God and further His Kingdom. This diminishing of faith leads to a secular worldview.

Satan is the ultimate deceiver. Listen to how the apostle John warns believers to counter the devil's deception: *Dear children, do not let anyone lead you astray. The one who does what is right is righteous, just as he is righteous. The one who does what is sinful is of the devil, because the devil has been sinning from the beginning. The reason the Son of God appeared was to destroy the devil's work* (1 John 3:7–8). To further his deception, the Devil puts blinders on those outside the faith so they cannot see truth – *The god of this age has blinded the minds of unbelievers, so that they cannot see the light of the gospel that displays the glory of Christ, who is the image of God* (2 Corinthians 4:4).

Clearly, those leading the secular agenda in America do not have in mind the concerns of God. The works of the devil are to counter the work of God. As a murderer, Satan works against God, who is Life. As a liar, Satan works against God, who is Truth. In the lives of unbelievers, the work of the devil is to keep them from coming to saving faith in Christ. In the lives of believers, the work of the devil is to tempt us to sin and thus blunt our witness to Christ in the world, and deny us the joy of thriving.

The encouragement for believers is this: *You, dear children, are from God and have overcome them, because the one who is in you is greater than the one who is in the world. They are from the world and therefore speak from the viewpoint of the world, and the world listens to them. We are from God, and whoever knows God listens to us; but whoever is not from God does not listen to us. This is how we recognize the Spirit of truth and the spirit of falsehood* (1 John 4:4-6).

The Remedy for our Plight

What do I suggest to remedy the lawlessness in our land, and the persecution it brings to believers? The only solution that gets to the root of the problem is a heart transplant – where the love of God draws people to seek, know and follow Jesus. Pastor Tim Keller said, "Our society is secularizing, and Christianity seems to be in long-term decline. But renewal is possible."[39] It certainly is! *And this is the testimony: God has given us eternal life, and this life is in his Son. Whoever has the Son has life; whoever does not have the Son of God does not have life* (1 John 5:11-12).

When the crowd in the Apostle Peter's time asked what they should do in response to the corruption in their generation, Peter did not suggest more security in schools, better gun control, or more cameras posted on street corners. No, *Peter replied, 'Repent and be baptized, every one of you, in the name of Jesus Christ for the forgiveness of your sins; and you will receive the gift of the Holy Spirit.'* Peter went on to say that, *this promise is for you and your children and for all who are far off—for all the Lord our God will call* (Acts 2:38-39). That includes you and me!

We hear the phrase, "Separation of church and state" and are told that that our faith should be private – that we shouldn't impose our faith on others or apply it to the laws of the land. Nothing could be further from the truth. Our founding fathers believed the moral code consistently laid out in the Bible should be the foundation upon which our laws, our rights, and our constitution are based. As a nation America was, and I hope still is, united "In God We Trust."

In Summary

The Apostle Paul warns us to...*not be outwitted by Satan; for we are not ignorant of his designs* (2 Corinthians 2:11).

Here is how Satan works according to the Bible:

1. He blinds the minds of unbelievers – *The god of this age has blinded the minds of the unbelievers, to keep them from seeing the light of the gospel of the glory of Christ* (2 Corinthians 4:4). So he not only speaks what is false, he also hides what is true. Satan keeps us from seeing the treasure of the gospel; the Pearl of Great Price.

2. He lies and is the Father of Lies – John says that Satan has nothing to do with the truth, because there is no truth in him (John 8:44). John Piper says of Satan, "We are dealing with the essence of falsehood and deception."[40]

3. Satan masquerades as an angel of light – *It is not surprising, then, if his servants also masquerade as servants of righteousness* (2 Corinthians 11:14-15).

4. He is deceitful – *I am afraid that as the serpent deceived Eve by his cunning, your thoughts will be led astray from a sincere and pure devotion to Christ* (2 Corinthians 11:3).

The good news is, GOD WINS! *And the devil who had deceived them was thrown into the lake of fire and sulfur where the beast and the false prophet were, and they will be tormented day and night forever and ever* (Revelation 20:10).

Martin Luther is credited with pinning the following statement to the Wittenberg door as part of his 95 theses: "If I profess with the loudest voice and clearest exposition every portion of the truth of God except precisely that little point which the world and the devil are at the moment attacking, I am not confessing Christ, however boldly I may be professing Christ. Where the battle rages, there the loyalty of the soldier is proved and to be steady on all the battle front besides, is mere flight and disgrace if he flinches at that point."

Let Us Stand Strong

No one has made a more profound impact on the world than Jesus of Nazareth, yet He was severely persecuted. The early Apostles were enormously effective in growing the Church. However, all but one of these early disciples was also martyred for their faith. Believers need to STEP UP and STAND FIRM in their faith. We cannot accept a status quo that relegates God, or His church, to the cheap seats. This stance may not make us popular and we will likely experience persecution to a greater degree than ever before. Following Jesus was not easy then and will not be today; that is, if we are willing to be honest and bold in our following. We do so because it's all true!

Questions to Consider

1. When have you experienced some form of persecution for your beliefs? How did this feel, and how did you handle it?

2. How should you prepare to overcome persecution? What do you need to fortify yourself?

3. In what way might you go on offense to overcome the attacks of faith in our culture?

CHAPTER 22

Avoid Getting Stuck in a Rut

So let us know, let us PRESS ON
to know the Lord!
Hosea 6:3

Therefore confess your sins to each other and
pray for each other so that you may be healed.
The prayer of a righteous person
is powerful and effective.
James 5:16

I was recently challenged by a stinging question: Might my following of Jesus have become formulaic? I have done a considerable amount of four-wheeling in sand and know what it's like to get entrenched in a rut so deep that the Jeep stays on track even if I let go of the wheel. I wonder if my journey with Jesus can get stuck in a comfortable rut? Could my devotional life have become so formulaic that it is running practically on auto pilot?

Spinning our Wheels

I love rotaries because they negate the need for yet another stinkin' traffic light! The granddaddy rotary of them all is the Arc de Triumph in Paris. We lived there for a year and relished taking visiting Americans for a Death Ride around this circle. If memory serves me, there are nineteen lanes of traffic encircling the monument, and twelve roads entering and exiting.

The goal is to get around the rotary and keep moving toward the desired destination. But with all those lanes of traffic merging the same direction, it can be difficult to cut through to exit. When this happens one is forced to drive around the circle again hoping for a break in the traffic the next time by. I wonder what the world record is for the most laps someone made while trying to exit? But I digress…

Rotaries give us the sensation we are always moving, but in actuality, they can keep us stuck in a holding pattern and keep us from making progress. We've all experienced being on an airplane and heard the announcement come on the loudspeaker, "Prepare for landing." The plane circles the airport until it is vectored in to a clear runway to land. I've been on flights where this final circling of the airport has continued for over an hour.

I postulate that many of our life routines have a similar affect. We have our morning routines, our weekend routines, our comfortable patterns to help navigate our week. We have our comfortable style of devotions, our oft traveled routes and food stops. But if we are not challenged to use our gifts, stretch our faith, get out of our comfort zones, and put into practice what we are learning, then we, too, are merely in a holding pattern. Like my agronomist daughter always says, if a plant stops growing it is beginning to die. The same is true for our souls.

Not only do we have ingrained spiritual habits, but we are susceptible to the presence of habitual sins that make us feel stuck in our relationship with Jesus. Just when we break loose and take three steps forward, we stumble and fall back to where we started – or at least that's what it feels like. But these snares did not sneak up on the Lord – He knew they would come and He gives us what we need to persevere. In fact, Jesus has been praying for our victory all along – *Satan has asked to sift you as wheat. But I have prayed for you, [insert your name], that your faith may not fail* (Luke 22:21-32).

Listen to this faith-filled prayer of David: *Keep steady my steps according to your promise, and let no iniquity get dominion over me* (Psalm 119:133). Steady steps imply a journey forward toward a destination. David did not want obstacles, like complacency or habitual sin, to get in his way.

I begin each day in prayer and personal Bible study and fall asleep at night thanking the Lord for the day that has passed. I strive to love my neighbors and be a witness where I can. My wife and I attend church as often as possible, and we are available for ministry rolls as called upon. But is that all there is to following the Lord of Life?

While rhythms can be good (solitude and community, work and rest, stillness and action, silence and spoken word, engagement and retreat), if we allow them to become formulaic we deprive ourselves of their full power. We don't want to build reflex actions that allow us to go through our daily motions without having to apply thought, faith and intention. This is one of the gifts brought to us by the various seasons of the Church – Advent, Lent, etc. They bring a fresh focus to break up our spiritual routines.

Let's examine our prayer lives for a moment. In the Sermon on the Mount Jesus said, *When you pray, do not use vain repetitions as the heathen do. For they think that they will be heard for their many words* (Matthew 6:7). Jesus is warning us that simply repeating phrases known by heart will not help us be heard by God. In fact, He even says that formulaic praying is what the Heathens do! The prophet Isaiah concurs: God says, *These people come near to me with their mouth and honor me with their lips, but their hearts are far from me* (Isaiah 29:13).

Jesus was anything but predictable. Notice some of the different ways He healed people: He spoke a dead girl back to life, He used spittle and mud to heal the eyes of a blindman, and He allowed a bleeding woman to simply touch his cloak. Like his healing styles, walking with Jesus is a dynamic, exciting and ever-changing journey. His disciples didn't know what to expect next, and neither should we.

Spiritual Cross-Training

Cross-training is great for our bodies. It keeps muscles from becoming so used to one way of movement that they cease to grow or stretch. Jesus invites us to cross-train spiritually as He continues to sanctify us and make us like himself.

For the past year and a half, I have been following a workout regimen that includes bike riding, core exercise, and some pushups (forgive me gals if I am causing you to stumble!) Last week, I played my first match of doubles Pickleball, which seemed like a fairly innocuous sport with minimal running. The next day my body complained loudly – I was sore from head to toe! Why? Was Pickleball more strenuous than my usual workout routine? Not at all. It just involved the use of different muscles and movements. I had forged a groove that was comfortable – Pickleball drew me out of my groove!

Many of us have well-hewn routines for our spiritual lives which are to be commended. But it is possible to get in a groove that, while exercising certain spiritual muscles, allows others to atrophy. This means our groove has become a rut! We never want this dynamic journey with the Lord to become run-of-the mill. We should be captivated by Jesus' presence each day, and this is possible with some spiritual cross-training.

Here are a few ideas you might intersperse in your rhythms to keep your relationship with the Lord dynamic:

- Prayer – Some days follow a prayer list, but allow some open days to sit quietly and let the Spirit guide your prayers. Once you come into the Lord's presence just be quiet and listen. You might also change up your posture when praying – sitting with open hands on knees, lying prostrate, kneeling, or walking.

- Bible reading – Sometimes read slowly and dive deep in your study. At other times, set a goal to read through a section of the Bible quickly to get a view from 30,000 feet. Each offers different levels of value. You may want to insert into your rhythm some Lectio Divina, where the Scriptures are a means to come into the presence of the Lord. Then you stop reading and simply enjoy His presence, responding to him prayerfully as you feel led.

- Praying the Scriptures – Take a month and read a Psalm and a Proverb each day and allow them to launch into a time of worship.

- Serve – Instead of serving in the areas where you are naturally gifted, step out of your comfort zone to serve where you must depend on the Lord for strength. I feel confident working with kids but homeless people make me uncomfortable. Perhaps they should be my next foray into service.

- Witness – Write out your testimony and look for one person with whom to share it. You may not often have the chance to share your whole story, but if you know the whole thing you can look for opportunities to insert portions of your story into conversations.

- Scripture Memory – Commit to a scripture memory plan or write down some passages you'd like to memorize. The Topical Memory System by NavPress is a great tool for this. I highly commend it!

- Take a Challenge – Commit to a 30-day quiet time challenge with a friend(s), where if one misses a day you both must start over!

- Worship by Singing – Sing some worship songs to the Lord as your audience of one.

- Spiritual Direction – Sign on to some sessions with a spiritual director (I'm available – rbeckwith80@gmail.com)

Another key for avoiding feeling stuck in a rut is to practice regular confession and repentance. While this is a sacrament for our Catholic brethren, it is too often treated as optional by protestants. Each time we pray the Lord's Prayer we ask Him to forgive our trespasses, but it is a general rather than specific mention of just what those trespasses were. It can also be healthy to confess our sins to a trusted brother or sister in Christ (James 5:16). The result of our confession is absolution from sin – the slate is wiped clean!

Most people struggle to completely forgive those who have grieved them. We may want to move on in these relationships and put the offense behind us, yet the memory of the pain it caused remains. God is not like that. Not only does He promise to forgive us, but to forget the sin once it is confessed – *For I will forgive their wickedness and will remember their sins no more* (Jeremiah 31:34). When we fall on our knees and confess "Lord, I did it again." He responds, "Did what?" That is the grace of our Lord!

Overcoming Inertia with Intentionality

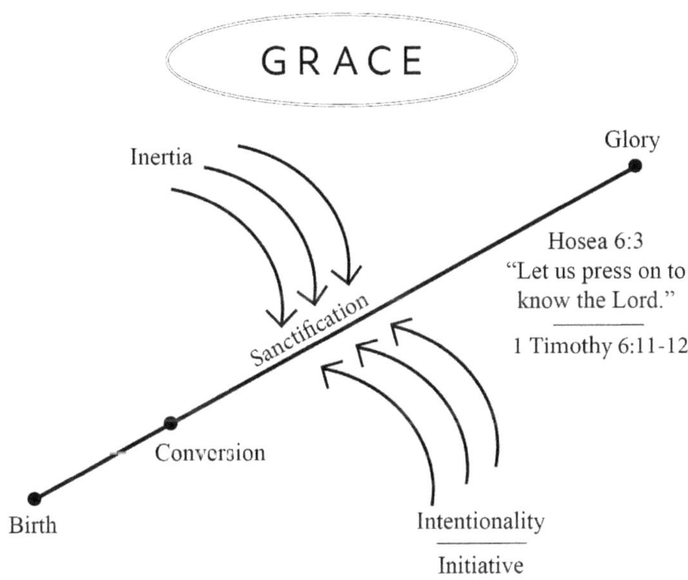

Inertia – "the tendency of a body to preserve a state of rest unless acted upon by an external force (The British Dictionary)."

Intentionality – "an attitude of purposefulness, with a commitment to deliberate action (Dictionary.com)." It is the best antidote to inertia!

As discussed earlier, the phase of salvation that occurs between our conversion and our glorification in heaven is called, "sanctification" – the process of growing more and more into the image of Jesus. Inertia is a law of physics that asserts pressure on things to remain as they are. Rather than being a catalyst for growth, inertia is an impediment to personal transformation. This property is a tool in the devil's hand to deprive believers of the joy of growing closer to Jesus a bit more each day, each week, each month, and each year.

How is inertia overcome? By disciplining ourselves to be intentional to seek growth in Christ. It means learning to see Jesus in the center of every facet of our lives. It means seeking accountability and close fellowship with friends who spur us on. It means changing up our routines to stay flexible and sharp. The spiritual armor described in Ephesians 6 should be engaged to arm ourselves against the devil's schemes. Being intentional means sitting under sound teaching at church and experiencing soul-filling worship. And, it means finding our gifts and applying them to the service of others. We knock out inertia when we GET ON MISSION!

Pause and Reflect

I suggest you pause your reading here and do a little journaling…

Think back over your journey with Jesus and note a few standout experiences that caused lasting growth. Some of these happened merely by chance, but others may be repeatable. See what steps you come up with for ramping up your growth curve! We are only on this earth for a millisecond in the scope of eternity so, *Let us know, let us PRESS ON to know the Lord* (Hosea 6:3, emphasis added).

Avoiding Spiritual Drift

What is wrong with this picture? What is this bear lacking that it needs for survival? Just as we need the six essentials in the left column to survive physically, we also need the six corresponding essentials in the right column to thrive spiritually.

Food	→	God's Word
Water	→	Prayer
Community	→	Fellowship Affirmation
Purpose	→	Eternal purpose/calling
Reproduction	→	Mission/witness
Shelter	→	Church

When a believer lacks any of these critical needs, they begin to drift. Of the investments in your journey that have had a lasting impact, which spiritual essential do they fall under? I will highlight just three from my journey…

First, following my senior year of high school and my recent introduction to a personal relationship with Jesus, I was serving on the work crew at Young Life's camp Saranac in upstate New York. Each week the work crew boss would ask one of the work crew to share their testimony with the campers during one of the evening club meetings. I was terrified he might choose me as I had no idea what I would say. Thankfully, I made it through all four weeks without being picked; phew! However, there was still the last weekend of the summer which was an adult camp. My parents would be attending since they had to pick me up to drive me to college right afterwards.

Sure enough, Chip, the work crew boss, came to me and asked if I would like to share my testimony. I politely declined saying that it would be awkward with my parents there. Chip retorted, "That is why I'm asking you." I told him no, but thanked him for thinking of me. Then Chip pulled the guilt card and said, "I prayed about it and I think you are supposed to share." "OK!" I yelled. So my buddy John and I headed off to the lean-to to work on what I should say. We filled 8 legal pages with notes for my three-minute speech!

That evening I was introduced to share and said nothing of what I had prepared. At the end of that meeting, the camp speaker offered the chance for anyone who had begun a personal relationship with Jesus that weekend to stand and say so. To my amazement, my mother stood up. Following the meeting, my father, who was a former college football player and somewhat of a tough guy, came up to me and said, "Son, I'm not into all that standing up stuff, but ME TOO!" This first hand, awe inspiring experience with my testimony showed me the power of God at work in our meager stories. When we avail ourselves to be used by Him He shows up in big ways. God loves to be trusted.

My dad passed away a couple of years ago and I was privileged to speak at his memorial service. Some find it odd I have hardly shed a tear since his passing because I know he is with the Lord in paradise. Were he not a believer I would grieve his loss every day. God got dad's attention through a number of means, my testimony being one. That experience has fueled my passion to share Jesus with others.

The second investment came when I decided to accept the area director position for Young Life in Fairfax, Virginia. My life-long buddy, John, had been living in New Jersey since college, but as soon as I told him I was going to plant a ministry to teens in Fairfax he quit his job and moved down here to be in it with me. He has been a constant source of guidance and encouragement, and has kept me accountable to growing in my walk with Jesus. John's sacrificial investment in me demonstrated what true fellowship is all about.

The last investment I'll share came from my first boss in Young Life, Chuck Reinhold. When I joined the Young Life staff at age 24, Chuck informed his staff that he wanted to give us a gift. We were thinking gift cards to a trendy restaurant would be nice, but no! The gift was a 90-Day Challenge to commit to beginning each of the next 90 days with an hour of scripture reading and prayer, and listening to the Lord for applications. For accountability, he threw in that if any one of the 20 of us missed a day, we would ALL have to start the 90 days over again! (He wasn't kidding!)

While it took our group more than 90 days to complete the challenge; we did it, and this experiment in God's Word built in me the most life-transforming habit anyone can acquire. I now begin each day with a time in the Scriptures and prayer and ask the Lord to build my game plan for each day. I hate to ever miss!

Often it is difficult to perceive when our lives are beginning to "drift" from intimate dependence on Jesus. When work and relationships are running on all cylinders we feel less of a need to come to the Lord on our knees for the wisdom, guidance, and rich fellowship Jesus offers. The old frog in the kettle illustration is certainly true. Like warm water, ease in life can lull us into complacency before we are boiled alive. This is why it is essential to have habits (and friends) in place that keep us pressed to Jesus and focused on His kingdom. Whether things are going well or we are struggling, we have a foundation on which to stand that cannot be shaken.

To sum up, Dallas Willard encourages a three-fold pattern believers should follow if they want to experience personal transformation: Vision, Intention, and Means.[41]

> A. **Vision** – we must first have a vision or mental picture of what we want to become. What qualities do we seek, what do we look like living out these qualities, and how will we be different than we are now? This vision must be realistic when sprinkled with faith so that, with the help of the Spirit, we believe it will be attained. It is also important to clearly state the benefits of attaining such a vision.
>
> B. **Intention** – set goals to reach the vision, and set up benchmarks for progress. Find a friend to encourage and hold you accountable to your goals.
>
> C. **Means** – the spiritual disciplines and armor for battle. What tools will you employ to succeed?

I'll close with this assuring prayer from the Apostle Paul:

> *For this reason, since the day we heard about you, we have not stopped praying for you. We continually ask God to fill you with the knowledge of his will through all the wisdom and understanding that the Spirit gives, so that you may live a life worthy of the Lord and please him in every way: bearing fruit in every good work, growing in the knowledge*

of God, being strengthened with all power according to his glorious might so that you may have great endurance and patience, and giving joyful thanks to the Father, who has qualified you to share in the inheritance of his holy people in the kingdom of light. For he has rescued us from the dominion of darkness and brought us into the kingdom of the Son he loves, in whom we have redemption, the forgiveness of sins (Colossians 1:9-14).

Between now and glory we are enjoying the process of being sanctified as we get to know Jesus better and take on his character one step at a time. Let's never get stuck in a rut because it's all true!

Questions to Consider

1. Have you allowed inertia to sap your growth in Christ? What might have contributed to this?

2. What experiences have caused you lasting growth in your life with Christ? Are there principles that can be applied going forward? What would you teach a younger believer in this regard?

3. What intentional steps will you employ to catalyze your spiritual life? Note these in My Plan for Thriving.

CHAPTER 23

Build a Library of Verses Committed to Memory

Keep this Book of the Law always on your lips; meditate on it day and night, so that you may be careful to do everything written in it. Then you will be prosperous and successful.
Joshua 1:8

All Scripture is God-breathed and is useful for teaching, rebuking, correcting and training in righteousness, so that the servant of God may be thoroughly equipped for every good work.
2 Timothy 3:16-17

When I joined the staff of Young Life in 1982, one of the required training assignments was to learn the Topical Memory System (TMS) developed by the Navigators. It is an ingenious system comprised of sixty verses, with twelve verses in each of five packs – Live the New Life, Proclaim Christ, Rely on God's Resources, Be Christ's disciple, and Grow in Christlikeness. The assignment was to learn two verses per week and to learn them word perfectly.

Thanks to the memory pegs and repetition I still know these verses by heart now four decades later. And, because they are at my beckon call, they come to mind frequently when teaching or mentoring people, or when I just need some direction myself. If I had not committed them to memory, I doubt these verses would come to mind for frequent application. I wish I had the capacity (or discipline!) to memorize the entire Bible!

Over the years I have accumulated a running list of "Life Verses" that I review monthly. Some I have committed to memory and others I haven't. They remind me of my identity, my unique calling, my specific mission, and the love God has for me.

Moses certainly understood the value of making God's Word part of the fabric of the Israelites. Listen to this exhortation: *And you must commit yourselves wholeheartedly to these commands that I am giving you today. Repeat them again and again to your children. Talk about them when you are at home and when you are on the road, when you are going to bed and when you are getting up. Tie them to your hands and wear them on your foreheads as reminders. Write them on the doorposts of your house and on your gates* (Deuteronomy 6:6-9).

We tend to grossly underestimate our ability to memorize. Some of you were likely tempted to skip past this chapter because Scripture memorization seems so arduous – am I right? This is a reflection of our time. Hebrew children were required to memorize the Pentateuch (the first five books of the Bible) by age 10 – that is 5845 verses! How did they do it? The community made this a priority. They put God's Law to song, they recited key texts before they ate and during various ceremonies, they placed verses on their foreheads in phylacteries, and were taught God's Word in school.

Today, community support for Scripture memorization is grossly deficient by comparison, but it can be done and is of great value for individuals and families who set their mind to it.

Why Memorize Scripture When I Have a Bible at My Beckon Call?

Why is memorizing Scripture of value? After all, we have access to the entire Bible right on our phones. Isn't that sufficient? Here are just a few benefits to memorizing Scripture:

• When God's words get planted in our memory, they become part of our thinking and shape our perspective. They can be called upon at any time.

• The Scriptures are a shield against temptation: *How can a young person stay on the path of purity? By living according to your word. I have hidden your word in my heart that I might not sin against you* (Psalm 119: 9, 11).

• God's Word equips us for spiritual warfare – *Take the helmet of salvation and the sword of the Spirit, which is the Word of God* (Ephesians 6:17).

• It fuels our witness to others – *Always be prepared to give an answer to everyone who asks you to give the reason for the hope that you have* (1 Peter 3:15b).

• Knowing the Word of God can make our prayer life even more effective: *If you abide in Me, and My words abide in you, you will ask what you desire, and it shall be done for you* (John 15:7).

Once when my old boss, Chuck Reinhold, was returning to Washington, DC from Ethiopia, he arrived completely dehydrated. They also discovered that this former Pitt all-American football player had developed a form of sports induced dementia that was starting to kick in. The result was when he landed he didn't know his name, address, phone number, or even his wife's name. They immediately took him to the emergency room to try and diagnose the problem. While lying in the hospital bed confused about his whereabouts, the one thing Chuck remembered were his Topical Memory System Bible verses. His anxious heart was comforted by repeating God's Word to himself because he knew it was all true. What a testimony to the power of Scripture memory!

As we grow in our sanctification, we gradually take on more and more of a Kingdom lens through which to view life. Our heart begins to be moved by the causes that moved Jesus' heart. Memorizing God's Word greases our sanctification process. The Apostle John reminds us that, *In the beginning was the Word, and the Word was with God, and the Word was God* (John 1:1). Then he names who the Word is: *And the Word became flesh and lived among us, and we have seen his glory, the glory as of a father's only son, full of grace and truth* (John 1:14). If Jesus is the Word, does it not behoove us to drink deeply from it – even to the point of memorizing key verses?

Proverbs 7:2-3 says, *Keep my commands and you will live; guard my teachings as the apple of your eye. Bind them on your fingers; write them on the tablet of your heart.* The tablet of our heart is different from our electronic tablets. The Scriptures become a part of our core when committed to memory.

Questions to Consider

1. What do you feel is a responsible stewardship of the gift of God's Word? How does Scripture memory fit into this vision?

2. What do you see as some practical benefits to memorizing Scripture? What tools could help you with this?

3. What is one verse or passage you will commit to memorize and by what date?

________________ ________________

Verse Date

CHAPTER 24

Honor the Lord with Your Wealth

By J. Manning Herr

Manning Herr is the President of Alpha Strategies Corporation. He has been my friend and financial advisor for over forty years. Manning is unique in that he sees life through the prism of the Holy Scriptures and has made a study of what God says about giving and generosity. More importantly, Manning has lived what he has learned. He has built a very successful business by counseling his clients to follow Biblical principles for investing their funds. I am honored he would write this chapter for us!

Honor the Lord with your wealth, with the firstfruits of all your crops; then your barns will be filled to overflowing, and your vats will brim over with new wine.
Proverbs 3:9-10

Just as you excel in everything – in faith, in speech, in knowledge, in complete earnestness and in your love for us – see that you also excel in this grace of giving.
2 Corinthians 8:7

Jesus said, 'Do not store up for yourselves treasures on earth, where moth and rust destroy, and where thieves break in and steal. But store up for yourselves treasures in heaven, where moth and rust do not destroy, and where thieves do not break in and steal. For where your treasure is, there your heart will be also.

Matthew 6:19-21

John D. Rockefeller was the wealthiest American of all time and was once among the richest men in the world. As the founder and president of Standard Oil, he commanded 90% of the oil refined in the U.S by age 38. By 50, he was the richest man in the country. But at the age of 53 Rockefeller became deathly ill. He was in constant pain and his body seemed to be shutting down. He couldn't sleep, could barely eat, and he lost interest in his life's work and quest to gain more wealth. His doctors predicted he had no more than a year to live.

One morning during his failing state, Rockefeller came to the realization that he would not be able to take any of his money into the afterlife. For the first time, this strong business leader was not in control of his destiny. So he made a radical decision: he established the John D. Rockefeller Foundation that would invest his assets in building hospitals and doing research on various chronic diseases like Malaria and Tuberculosis. One notable fruit of this investment was the discovery of Penicillin.

A strange thing happened once he made this commitment to generosity: Rockefeller began healing physically. In fact, he lived to be 98 – forty-five years longer than his doctors had thought possible. Ebanye Christy notes, "Rockefeller discovered the power of gratitude and philanthropy, giving away the majority of his wealth. This act not only healed him but also made him whole."[42]

In his later years, Rockefeller reflected in his diary: "God taught me that everything belongs to Him, and I am merely a channel to fulfill His wishes."

Let's begin with why – why be generous? Through the lens of scripture you could argue that it is an act of obedience, and that would be true. But generosity is also an act of faith, trust and love. Being generous in specific ways outlined in Deuteronomy 14, 15, and 24 results in God's blessing on our vocation. In Malachi 3, God actually provokes the prophet to give and makes him this incredible promise: *'Bring the whole tithe into the storehouse, that there may be food in my house. Test me in this,' says the Lord Almighty, 'and see if I will not throw open the floodgates of heaven and pour out so much blessing that there will not be room enough to store it* (Malachi 3:10).'

The blessing that results from generosity will be so obvious that..*all the nations will call you blessed, for yours will be a delightful land, says the LORD Almighty* (Malachi 3:12). Generosity is a blessing for others that results in our own blessing by God. Each morning I pray, "Father, who would you have me bless today?"

While all of this is true, and I have acted in faith in response to these passages, it's not the core reason for my own generosity. The real reason I'm motivated to be generous is because I'm a Christian hedonist. I am selfish about my joy and being generous brings me an endless amount of intoxicating joy!

Arthur Brooks, using data on 30,000 American families, found that for every dollar a family gives to charity, their income increases on average by $3.75. He attributes this phenomenon to the psychological and social benefits of giving, such as increased happiness, stronger social networks, and greater opportunities, which can lead to long-term financial gains. Brooks also notes that giving can be viewed as an investment in a "virtuous cycle of giving and getting" that benefits individuals, communities, as well as the nation's economy.

How do you know if your generosity is having the intended effect of blessing others? One of the primary ways is it results in thanksgiving to God. It is an incredible privilege that God chooses us to be channels of His infinite generosity. Let's be grateful!

Another marker is that you forget what you've done. Generosity is about Jesus and His love for mankind, not about us. Everything we have comes from God and He is the owner of it all; we are merely stewards of His generosity. So no pats on the back are necessary when we give to someone in need.

Where Should We Give?

The scriptures are filled with examples but Jesus gets wonderfully specific in Matthew 25. In this passage He opens up for us the windows of heaven and shows us what will transpire when He takes His seat on His glorious throne. Jesus talks very specifically about the hungry, the thirsty, the foreigner, the naked, the sick and the prisoner. What His righteous children did was show simple acts of generosity towards each of these people groups.

How hard is it to give someone a drink or a meal? Our closets are overstuffed with clothing we never wear. It's pretty easy to bring a meal to a sick neighbor. I think the saints were incredulous that this is what Jesus talked about. He didn't talk about leading Bible studies or being an elder in a church. He didn't talk about the amount of giving either; just the recipients of our giving.

I have five specific ministries on which I focus a large percentage of my giving that target exactly what Jesus talked about in Matthew 25. Additionally, based on James 1:27, widows and orphans should be people to whom we show generosity.

I strongly encourage you to keep walking down the path of generosity. Pray for wisdom as you search the scriptures looking for insights and acts of generosity – they are on nearly every page. Ask God to bless you that you might be a blessing. My hope for you is that you would come to know the truth of 2 Corinthians 9:7 *...for God loves a cheerful giver.*

Why Should We Tithe?

Here are Eight Good Reasons:

1. It is an act of obedience honoring to the Lord
2. It provides for the work of the Church
3. It shows God we trust Him
4. It connects our money to a kingdom purpose
5. It gives our work eternal significance
6. It breaks the dual grips of greed and self-reliance
7. It signifies to everyone and anyone that God comes first
8. It blesses the giver as well as the receiver

Questions to Consider

1. Rate yourself on a scale of 1 to 5 regarding your current level of generosity. Do you feel like a generous person? What contributed to getting you to this point?

2. What is a cause that burdens you that you would like to help with either your time, treasure, or both?

3. Which of the Six Good Reasons to tithe motivate you?

*If you would like help investing your wealth wisely, you may reach out to Manning at: manning@alphastrategies.com

A Prayer from the Westminster Larger Catechism (WLC 147)

Giver of every good gift, offering you the first-fruits of what I make and produce is a good spiritual discipline that helps my heart wriggle free from the grip of my possessions and rest content. Keep me in that freedom, a radically generous life that joyfully furthers the good of your Kingdom. In the name of Jesus, amen.

CHAPTER 25

Protect your Wedding Vows

He answered, "Have you not read that he who created them from the beginning made them male and female, and said, 'Therefore a man shall leave his father and his mother and hold fast to his wife, and the two shall become one flesh'? So they are no longer two but one flesh. What therefore God has joined together, let not man separate."
Matthew 19:4-6

Let each one of you love his wife as himself, and let the wife see that she respects her husband.
Ephesians 5:33

Scripture clearly states that marriage was God's idea, not ours. Marriage and the raising of children in secure, loving homes is the lynchpin of a healthy society. When God's design for marriage is broken not only are individual families strained, but society suffers as well.

Let me say right up front that divorce happens. Jesus even offers some circumstances where divorce is permitted. If anyone reading this has gone through the turmoil of divorce please know that God's heart breaks for the pain you've experienced. It was not His plan. Lean into Him for comfort and guidance as you navigate your next chapters. He has not left you!

The ramifications of broken marriages and kids raised in fatherless homes are far reaching. Listen to these statistics:[43]

- 85% of youths in prison come from fatherless homes
- 71% of high school dropouts come from fatherless homes
- 90% of all homeless and runaway children are from fatherless homes
- 60% of youth suicides are from fatherless homes

The Heritage Foundation found that high-crime neighborhoods are characterized by high concentrations of families abandoned by fathers. Yet even in high-crime inner-city neighborhoods, well over 90 percent of children from stable two-parent homes do not become delinquents. By contrast only 10 percent of children from unsafe, unstable homes in these neighborhoods avoid crime.[44] These statistics do not say that kids born to single moms, or kids in families where the dad has left have no chance of thriving; they certainly do. It is just that the forces working against them are much greater so they require support from extended family, friends, and other community resources.

Why Not Marry?

2024 studies show that only 60% of thirty-five-year-old men are married today, while 90% of men in this age group were married in 1980.[45] The predicted continuing decline in marriage will have far-reaching consequences for our society at large.

Susan Brown, professor of Sociology and director of the Center for Family and Demographic Research at Bowling Green State University says, these days "There's a longer checklist of items you need to complete before you're considered marriageable. You need to get a real job. You need to be living independently. All of these milestones take time to achieve, and as we all know, many people aren't ever going to achieve them."[46]

Susan Brown's research highlights some practical reasons couples either wait or don't marry today. But what are some additional downsides, and why are less people choosing this route than ever?

We first must remind ourselves there are never actual downsides to following God's design. His Word and his directives are for our thriving, not our punishment. It should come as no surprise that the decline in the percentage of people getting married in this country follows the declining trend in both church attendance and belief in the Judeo-Christian God. The divorce rate is also representative of a decreasing commitment to these "religious" marriage vows.

Lois Collins, a family issues reporter for Dessert News, recently sponsored a national study on faith and relationships. Here is the heading of her findings: "A new report sees a strong link between men not going to church, marriage declines and struggling Christianity."[47] A 2018 American Social and Political Behavior Survey said those who grew up in an intact family are nearly twice as likely to go to church regularly compared to those who did not grow up with both parents at home.[48] What is not clear is which precipitated the other: do struggling marriages cause people to leave church, or is spiritual disinterest causing more folks to live together or never marry?

What is a Vow?

I have had the privilege to officiate dozens of weddings, mostly of former Young Life "kids." I love having a front row seat to see their faces as they stare longingly into each other's eyes and vow their devotion through thick or thin. But what exactly is a vow? We don't use that term in too many places these days.

A vow is a solemn promise made to God, and in the case of marriage, to and on behalf of the person we are marrying. It is a declaration of our firm commitment of all that we are to fulfill our pledge. Here is what the officiant typically asks the couple to repeat to one another: "In the name of God, I ____ take you, ____ to be my husband/wife, to have and to hold from this day forward, for better for worse, for richer, for poorer, in sickness and in health, to love and to cherish, until we are parted by death. This is my solemn vow."

What contingency is not covered in this vow? And, how long is it good for? Until death does us part. It makes sense then, in a culture with a declining level of commitment to Christ, that these vows would be treated as nice ideas, but not a promise before a Holy God. A proper view of any vow to the Lord, certainly the vow of our fidelity to follow Him for life, should be supported by regular goal setting, intentionality, accountability, mentoring, counseling, and whatever it takes to fulfill this high calling. Like a muscle, if our vows aren't exercised they will atrophy. Our marriages are no different. Here again, intentionality is key (see diagram in chapter 22)!

Like a muscle, if our vows aren't exercised they will atrophy.

Investing in our Vows

My wife and I married around the same time as several couples in our Young Life community here in Fairfax, Virginia. Since we were friends already it seemed quite natural to form a couples group as a means to support each other in our wedding vows. We met weekly to study the Bible, share stories, and pray for one another. When kids came on the scene we backed off to every other week and hired a baby sitter to watch the gang downstairs while we parents met upstairs. Now, thirty-eight years later, we are still in tight fellowship with this group. Even though there have been challenges with kids, money, work or extended family, all six couples are still together and thriving, thanks to God's grace!

It is essential we don't measure our marital health by the standards of the culture. Our measuring stick should be what the Lord says is possible and true. Paul presents an attractive picture of a healthy marriage in his first letter to the Corinthians: *Love is patient and kind; love does not envy or boast; it is not arrogant or rude. It does not insist on its own way; it is not irritable or resentful; it does not rejoice at wrongdoing, but rejoices with the truth. Love bears all things, believes all things, hopes all things, endures all things* (1 Corinthians 13:4-7). We do well to break this down phrase by phrase and make it our standard.

What are some practical ways we can invest in our marriage relationship and protect from slowly drifting apart?

1. Watch for slow leaks and plug them up (figure out what yours might be)

2. Know the work of the enemy so he doesn't sneak up on you (see chapter 16)

3. Resolve arguments quickly and forgive each other. Don't let petty disagreements fester.

4. Communicate regularly and well

5. Don't give up dating each other – be creative!

6. Find a few things you enjoy in common and plug them into your schedule

7. Don't walk alone – commit to some other couples and hold each other up

Rather than looking at marriage through fearful eyes because of the inherent challenges, let's lean in with hopeful expectancy, and a little wisdom to guide us along the way. As I tell couples I marry, there are actually three people being married on God's altar – there is the groom, the bride, and Jesus Christ who pledges his support and his presence always. *If God is for us, who can be against us* (Romans 8:31)? Because It's All True!

Questions to Consider

1. If you are married, how often do you review your vows? Do you feel like your relationship is growing, stagnant, or declining? Why?

2. What intentional step(s) will you take to invest in your marriage and affirm your vows? Plug these into My Plan for Thriving.

3. If unmarried, what is your view of marriage? What makes it attractive and/or unattractive? What will you do with these feelings?

CHAPTER 26

Be Thankful Always

Give thanks in all circumstances; for this is God's will for you in Christ Jesus.
1 Thessalonians 5:18

I will give thanks to the Lord with my whole heart; I will recount all of your wonderful deeds. I will be glad and exult in you; I will sing praise to your name, O Most High.
Psalm 9:1-2 (ESV)

I had the privilege to visit my former boss when he was near the end of his life in a nursing home and plagued by dementia. It felt so good to sit with him and hear him say, nearly continually, "I'm so thankful." I'm looking at a former All-American football star who lived a vibrant life now left just to stare at a TV with nothing of interest on it, in a stale hospital room. And he is thankful??? He told me he was thankful for his faithful wife, his fruit-filled life, for me visiting him, but mostly, Chuck was thankful he knew the Lord so well. His thanks was deep and sincere.

My dear friend Lou Martini survived pancreatic cancer years longer than doctors predicted. Lou walked with an attitude of gratitude. Instead of being bitter about his disease, Lou dwelt upon the incredible blessings he had enjoyed in this life: his family, his beloved employees, and many special friends in his inner circle. I visited Lou occasionally during his struggle with the effects of chemotherapy. My intent was to encourage this dear brother, but driving home I would always kick myself as I realized Lou had encouraged me instead. Lou practiced thanksgiving and I'm sure arrived in heaven with a beaming grin on his face!

The apostle Paul reflected a similar attitude despite having to endure more obstacles than any of us reading this could imagine. Listen to his journey – *Are they servants of Christ? I know I sound like a madman, but I have served him far more! I have worked harder, been put in prison more often, been whipped times without number, and faced death again and again. Five different times the Jewish leaders gave me thirty-nine lashes. Three times I was beaten with rods. Once I was stoned. Three times I was shipwrecked. Once I spent a whole night and a day adrift at sea. I have traveled on many long journeys. I have faced danger from rivers and from robbers. I have faced danger from my own people, the Jews, as well as from the Gentiles. I have faced danger in the cities, in the deserts, and on the seas. And I have faced danger from men who claim to be believers but are not. I have worked hard and long, enduring many sleepless nights. I have been hungry and thirsty and have often gone without food. I have shivered in the cold, without enough clothing to keep me warm. Then, besides all this, I have the daily burden of my concern for all the churches* (2 Cor 11:23-28).

It is painful just reading Paul's account of hardships! Despite all these challenges, Paul is still thankful and desirous to teach his church to walk with a thankful attitude. Listen for the key to overcoming anxiety Paul casually mentions in this verse: *Do not be anxious about anything, but in every situation, by prayer and petition, with thanksgiving, present your requests to God. And the peace of God, which transcends all understanding, will guard your hearts and your minds in Christ Jesus* (Philippians 4:6-7).

The apostle gives us two prescriptions for overcoming anxiety. The first is offering our specific petitions to the Lord in prayer. The second one is often overlooked but equally as powerful – *with thanksgiving*. Focusing on what is good, that for which we are grateful, is a proven prescription for overcoming anxiety. Here are just a few practical ways being thankful can impact our emotional state:

Focusing on what is good, that for which we are grateful, is a proven prescription for overcoming anxiety.

- It reminds us of God's goodness from past history
- It reminds us He is with us in our trials as well as in the good times – He gets us!
- It is a statement of faith that we practice thanksgiving even when we aren't feeling it
- It assures us that God loves us and is in control
- Thanksgiving honors the Lord and draws us to worship Him

Being thankful brings a sense of calm to our being. People who are highly driven toward success are anxious much of the time because they never fully arrive at an ultimate state of success – they are always looking ahead for something more. Being thankful makes us grateful for the blessings we have received. That does not mean we want to remain in this same place forever. Having ambition, godly ambition, is a good thing. But we can be thankful at each stop along the way rather than holding out for the climax.

Give Thanks as a Form of Worship

Enter his gates with thanksgiving; go into his courts with praise. Give thanks to him and praise his name (Psalm 100:4). Not only is being thankful good for our souls, it is also a form of worship when we thank God for His many blessings. God is honored when we take the time to thank Him for how we experience Him each day. The alternative is to take Him for granted or ignore His presence. A reading through the book of Psalms is wonderfully instructive for learning to praise the Lord, with thanksgiving.

Questions to Consider

1. What are you thankful for today…? How does it feel just bringing these blessings to mind?

2. Do you naturally share your gratitude for the people in your life? Why or why not?

3. How much do you practice "thanking the Lord" during your day?

4. How might you incorporate thanksgiving more into your daily rhythms? Add these to My Plan for Thriving.

Book Closing

Because It's All True

Jesus said, *Whoever is not with me is against me, and whoever does not gather with me scatters* (Matthew 12:30). If we are not actively pursuing Christ and His causes, growing in our relationship with Him, and praying with Him for the flourishing of our community, then we are unknowingly participating in the plans of the enemy.

John Mark Comer reminds us not to view following Jesus as a means to an end – a ticket to heaven or guaranteed path to personal fulfilment. He is the end Himself. The reward for following Jesus is Jesus.[49] Enjoy Him forever!

The prophet Hosea offers this exhortation to believers of every generation: *So let us know, let us PRESS ON to know the Lord* (Hosea 6:3, emphasis added). I pray as you are diligent with the applications you noted in My Plan for Thriving that you will experience greater intimacy with our Lord, and see unimaginable fruit in your life. Yes, you will thrive!

Take a few minutes to firm up your Plan for Thriving and begin plugging these Holy Spirit inspired actions into your schedule. Perhaps find a partner and share your list for accountability and encouragement.

Coaching Available

If you would be interested in a spiritual director or life coach to walk with you on your journey with Jesus, feel free to email me at: rbeckwith80@gmail.com.

I Wish You All God's best!

Rick

Appendix #1

My Plan for Thriving

CHAPTER	ACTION STEPS	BY DATE

My Plan for Thriving

CHAPTER	ACTION STEPS	BY DATE

My Plan for Thriving

CHAPTER	ACTION STEPS	BY DATE

APPENDIX #2

My Dynamic Story

1. What were you like before encountering Jesus personally?

2. How and why did you surrender to Him?

3. What changes has Jesus brought to your life?

4. What are you currently learning in your walk with Jesus?

5. Who is on your Prospect List for sharing your story?

APPENDIX #3

Approaching God Through the Insights of Proverbs 2 and the Holy Spirit

A simple guide for connecting with God through His Word and the Holy Spirit

Here is a quick guide to help you practice what we've learned about the Word of God and the Holy Spirit—so you can experience God's truth, His heart, and His presence as you sit with Him.

Before You Begin: Invite the Holy Spirit

1. Ask the Holy Spirit to guide you into all truth.

Prayer Starter:

"God, thank You for meeting with me. As I read Your Word, Holy Spirit, would You teach me and guide me into all truth?"

2. Ask the Holy Spirit to whisper what He hears from the Father and from Jesus.

Prayer Starter:

"Holy Spirit, open my ears to hear what the Father and Jesus want to speak to me about who You are and who I am."

3. Ask that your time glorifies the Father and the Son.

Prayer Starter:

"Holy Spirit, may this time in Your Word bring honor and glory to God the Father and God the Son. Shape my heart to love and reflect Jesus."

---

1. Accept God's Word
"My son, if you accept my words..."
— Proverbs 2:1

Prayer Starter:

"God, I believe Your Word is true. As I read today, help my heart and mind receive Your truth joyfully so it can take root and transform me."

If convicted:

"Father, thank You for revealing who You are and who I am. I receive Your truth with joy. Forgive me where I have lived contrary to Your ways. Help me walk in Your truth—transform my heart to be more like Yours."

2. Store Up His Commands
"...and store up my commands within you..."
— Proverbs 2:1
When Scripture speaks to you—don't move too quickly.

• Highlight or write down the verse.
• Memorize it.
• Meditate on it.

Prayer Starter:

"Lord, drive this truth deep into my heart. Make it part of me."

Helpful Practice:

Write the verse on a card to revisit throughout the day.

3. Apply Your Heart to Understanding
"...apply your heart to understanding..."
— Proverbs 2:2

Ask God:
• "How do You want me to live this?"
• "What step of obedience or change are You inviting me into today?"
Write down any insight or next step the Holy Spirit gives.

4. Call Out for Insight & Cry Aloud for Understanding
"...call out for insight and cry aloud for understanding..." — Proverbs 2:3

Invite the Holy Spirit—the Helper and Teacher—to open Scripture to you.

Questions to ask:

- "Lord, what does this mean?"
- "Why is this here?"
- "What are You drawing my heart toward?"

If confused or unsure:

1. Re-read slowly, in context.
2. Pray again for clarity.
3. After prayerful reflection, check a trusted commentary for confirmation.

Record any insights, reminders, or questions.

5. Look for God as We Might Look for Silver or Hidden Treasure

"...if you look for it as for silver..."
— Proverbs 2:4

Seek God expectantly—not rushed.

If nothing stands out:

- Read again slowly.
- Ask: "Holy Spirit, is there more You want to show me?"
- Continue reading until something settles or stirs your heart.

Some days Scripture hits immediately.
Some days truth unfolds slowly.
Both are holy.
Keep showing up. God meets the one who seeks.

Closing Prayer

"God, thank You for Your Word and for meeting with me. Holy Spirit, remind me of what You revealed today at just the right time. Help me walk in this truth and recognize Your presence with me throughout the day. In Jesus' name, amen."

Your Response to God

Use the space below to write a personal prayer based on what God showed you today.

(You may want to include: gratitude, repentance, a response to what God revealed, a request for strength or guidance, and a desire for God's presence to linger with you.)

My Prayer to the Lord

APPENDIX #4

Discerning Your Personal Mission—Who am I Uniquely in Christ?

Whether you turn to the right or to the left, your ears will hear a voice behind you, saying, "This is the way; walk in it"
Isaiah 30:21

1. What are some **favorite verses** of Scripture you might consider "Life Verses?" What do these tell you about the passions and focus the Lord has for your life?

2. **Discerning your Personal Mission Statement.** Answer ing these questions will give you a lens through which to evaluate job opportunities, extracurricular involvements, and long-range goals.

    - What past roles or accomplishments have you found especially fulfilling?
    - What causes are you most passionate about?
    - What do you enjoy doing most?

- What are you uniquely skilled at doing?
- Where have you demonstrated repeated fruitfulness?
- What aspects of your jobs most feed your inner energy?
- What gifts or talents do others affirm in you?
- Which of these gifts or talents are natural? Which ones are learned?
- What is your motivational spiritual gift (Romans 12)?
- Gifts often have a corresponding weakness. What might yours be? For example, if you are an exhorter, you might struggle with being overly critical of others who aren't perform ing up to your expectations.

Now, write a statement or short paragraph that encapsulates who you are and to what you feel led to give your life. This will be your dynamic **personal mission statement** that you tweak throughout your life.

END NOTES

1. Jay Stone. "Carrey's Been Busted." Ottawa Citizen, December 16, 2005, F1–F2. Ottawa, Ontario. Accessed via Newspapers.com.

2. Spencer Sherman. "How Much Is Enough?" *Well Being Magazine*, November 25, 2020.

3. The Barna Group. "New Metrics for Measuring What Matters: Flourishing People and Thriving Churches." Church and Faith, March 2, 2022.

4. "J. Hudson Taylor." GeorgeMuller.org. Accessed May 16, 2025.

5. World Opinions. "This Is How Religious Liberty Dies." October 28, 2024.

6 . Dhruv Khullar, M.D., M.P.P. "Finding Purpose for a Good Life—but Also a Healthy One." New York Times. New York, 2018.

7. Tony Evans. Tony Evans Speaks Out on Fasting. Chicago: Moody Press, 2000.

8. George Marsden. "Mother of Modern Evangelicalism: The Life and Legacy of Henrietta Mears." The Gospel Coalition Reviews, January 25, 2021.

9. Jeff Chamblee. "Title unknown." The Stand (American Family Association), September 2024

10. Diane Montagna. "Pope Leo Encourages French Civic Leaders to Unite Politics and Faith." *Catholic Vote*, August 28, 2025.

11. John Mark Comer. *Practicing the Way.* Colorado Springs: WaterBrook, January 2024.

12. Lauren Meyers. "A Look Inside the Devil's Playbook with The Screwtape Letters." *Word on Fire*, August 1, 2024.

13. Ann M. Callahan. "The Concept of Person in the Theology of Hans Urs von Balthasar." *Fordham Research Commons*, 1993.

14. The Barna Group. Reviving Evangelism. January 2019.

15. George Vaillant. "Triumphs of Experience." The Harvard Second Generation Study. Cambridge, MA: Harvard University, 2012.

16. James Emery White. "Becoming a Player." The Church and Culture Blog 20, no. 52 (June 27, 2024).

17. Charles Hodge. Commentary on the Epistle to the Ephesians. New York: Robert Carter and Brothers, 1856.

18. Audrey Barrick, "Survey: Christians Worldwide Too Busy for God," *Christian Post Reporter* (July 30, 2007).

19. Jake Meador, "The Misunderstood Reason Millions of Americans Stopped Going to Church," *The Atlantic* (July 29, 2023).

20. Rick Warren, "A Call to Radical Commitment." Purpose Driven Life Devotional, 1.1.08.

21. Rabbi David Schiff, "Teens and Torah, What is Authentic Community?" JewishInsider, The Circuit (November 1, 2022).

22. John Mark Comer, *Practicing the Way* (Colorado Springs: Waterbrook Press, 2024), 160.

23. The National Study of Youth and Religion, Dr. Christian Smith, 2001-2006.

24. Apollo Technical, "Career and Hiring Advice," Ryan Bradshaw, March 14, 2024, web article.

25. Dave Alpern, "Taking the Lead," Tyndale, 2001, p.34.

26. Kara Powell, "Faith Beyond Youth Group," Fuller Youth Institute, Baker Books, 2023, p.59.

27. Timothy Witmer, Place for Truth, 'Things that Bug Me: Church Planters are Shepherds, Too." The Shepherd Leader, November 18, 2015.

28. J. Oswald Sanders, Knowing and Doing, Must Reads: Holy Spirit, September 3, 2004.

29. R.V.G. Tasker, The Line of Fire, You are the Salt of the Earth, May 17, 2022.

30. John Samson, Effectual Grace, January 2011.

31. R.C. Sproul, "The Law of Liberty," January 23, 2005.

32. "Explore by the Book," John 14-17, Romans and James, the Good Book Company, 2017, p.236.

33. Knowing and Doing, a publication of the C.S. Lewis Institute, Winter 2008.

34. Jake Meador, "The Misunderstood Reason Millions of Americans Stopped Going to Church," *The Atlantic*, July 29, 2023.

35. D. L. Moody, Golden Counsels, United Society of Christian Endeavor, 1889. Found on WholesomeWords.com.

36. John Mark Comer, *The Ruthless Elimination of Hurry*, Waterbrook, 2019, p.172.

37. Missy Takano, "What Is the Sabbath in the Bible and Should Christians Observe It? An Invitation to Holy Rest," *The Bible Project*, Jan 6, 2020.

38. John Mark Comer, *Practicing the Way*, PRH Christian Publishing, 2024, p.16.

39. Tim Keller, "American Christianity Is Due for a Revival," *The Atlantic*, Feb 5, 2023.

40. John Piper, *Desiring God*. "Resist the Devil," January 1, 1989.

41. Dallas Willard, "Renovation of the Heart," Nav Press, December 2021.

42. Ebenye Christy, Facebook post, John #Richest #wealth #Billionaire #fb #fbpost, 2024 #givingback #returnoninvestment #philanthropy #Philanthropist #philanthropic #foundationwork).

43. No Longer Fatherless, "Statistics on Fatherlessness in America and the Profound Impact Of Mentoring, Nolongerfatherless.org

44. Patrick Fagan, "The Real Root Causes of Violent Crime: The Breakdown of Marriage, Family, and Community," Heritage Foundation Report on Crime and Justice, March 17, 1995.

45. Lyman Stone, "1-in-3: A Record Share of Young Adults Will Never Marry," Institute for Family Studies, Feb 26, 2024.

46. Daniel De Vise, "Americans are waiting longer and longer to get married," *The Hill,* June 5, 2023.

47. Lois Collins, "Why fewer marriages, lower levels of faith are related," *Dessert News*, October 22, 2023.

48. *Ibid*

49. John Mark Comer, *Practicing the Way,* Random House, January 16, 2024, pgs. 52-53.

Image Sources:
Author created
FreePik
Google Free Images

About the Author

Rick Beckwith has served on the staff of Young Life for forty years in a variety of roles including, Sr. Regional Director for Metropolitan Washington, and Vice President of Strategic Initiatives. He has consulted with both for profit and nonprofit leaders across Europe as well as in Canada and the U.S. Rick's unique strengths are in growing things – people, companies, projects, and visions. Rick's first book, "What If It's All True" has received wide acclaim.

Rick is also an IAP certified life coach. He earned his B.A. from Denison University and M.A. in Theology from Fuller Theological Seminary. He and his wife, Kris, reside in the Washington, DC suburbs. They have three married daughters and six wonderful grandchildren.

When not working Rick can be found cheering on the Washington Capitals hockey team. "Let's go Caps!!!"

You might also enjoy Rick's book, *What If It's All True: Investigating the Person and Promises of Jesus*. To order, please scan the QR Code.

WHAT IF IT'S ALL TRUE?

9 781967 283040